ENDANGERED EARTH

ENDANGERED
EARTH

Anna Claybourne

Steve Parker

Miles
KeLLY

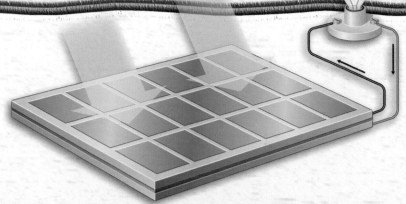

First published in 2011 by Miles Kelly Publishing Ltd
Harding's Barn, Bardfield End Green, Thaxted, Essex, CM6 3PX, UK

Copyright © Miles Kelly Publishing Ltd 2011

This edition printed 2013

2 4 6 8 10 9 7 5 3

Publishing Director Belinda Gallagher
Creative Director Jo Cowan
Editorial Director Rosie McGuire
Editors Carly Blake, Sarah Parkin
Cover Designer Simon Lee
Designers Joe Jones, Andrea Slane
Additional Design Kayleigh Allen
Image Manager Liberty Newton
Indexer Marie Lorimer
Production Manager Elizabeth Collins
Reprographics Stephan Davis, Jennifer Hunt, Ian Paulyn
Assets Lorraine King

ISBN 978-1-84810-467-9

Printed in China

British Library Cataloguing-in-Publication Data
A catalogue record for this book is available from the British Library

Made with paper from a sustainable forest

www.mileskelly.net
info@mileskelly.net

www.factsforprojects.com

CONTENTS

SAVING THE EARTH

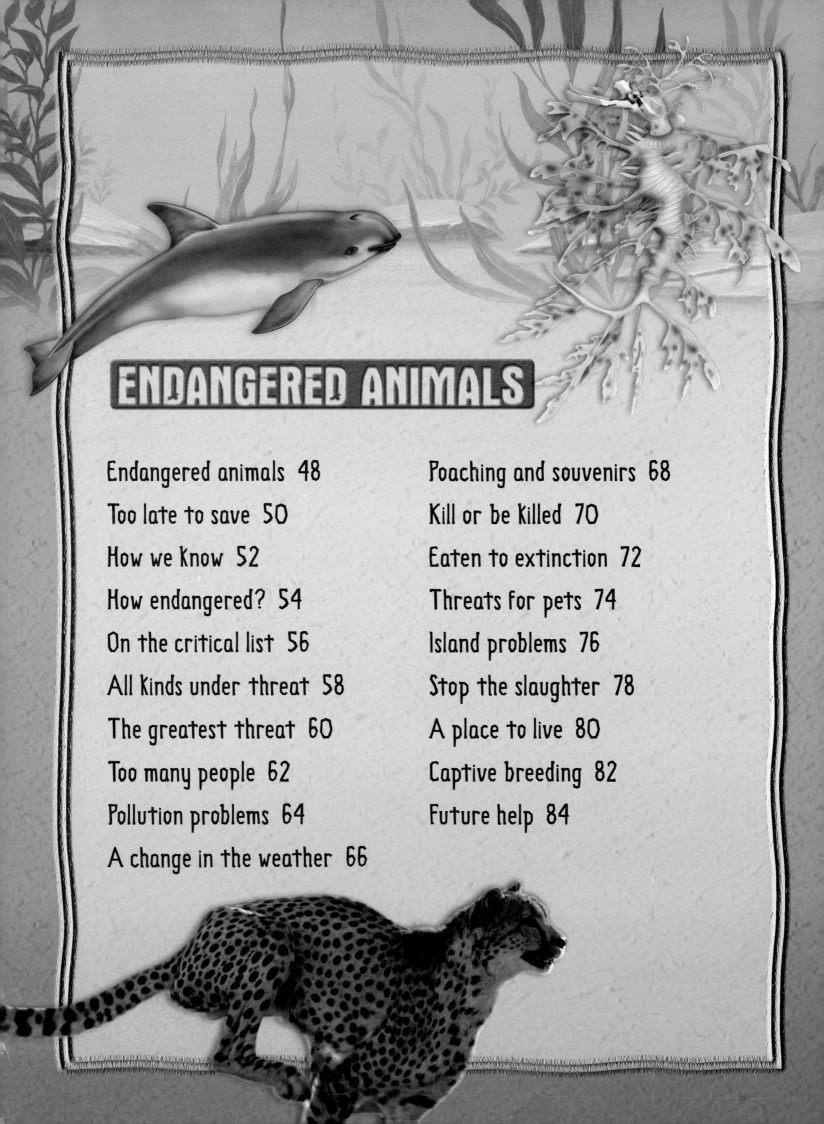

ENDANGERED ANIMALS

EXTINCT

SAVING THE EARTH

Our planet is in a mess! Humans have done more damage to the Earth than any other species. We take over land for farms, cities and roads, we hunt animals until they die out and we produce waste and pollution. Gases from cars, power stations and factories are changing the atmosphere and making the planet heat up. By making a few changes to live in a 'greener' way, we can try to save our planet.

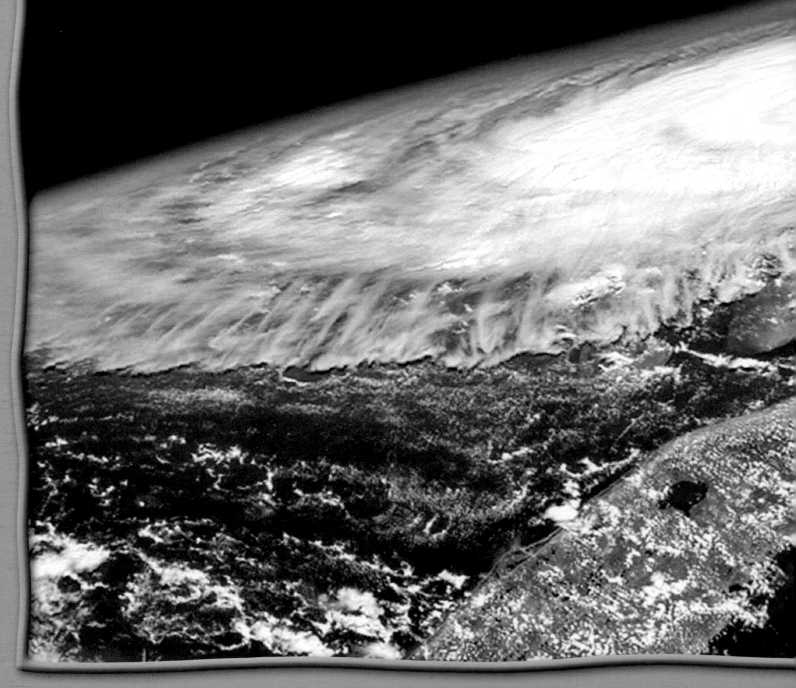

▼ As pollution makes the Earth warm up, more powerful storms form over the sea. This satellite photo shows Hurricane Frances moving over the Caribbean in 2004.

Global warming

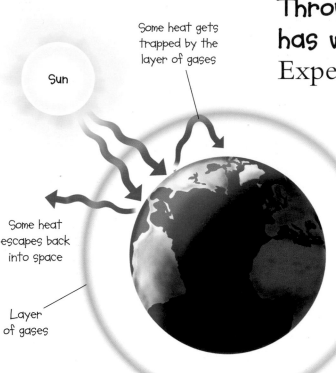

Some heat gets trapped by the layer of gases

Sun

Some heat escapes back into space

Layer of gases

Throughout its history, the Earth has warmed up and cooled down. Experts think that today's warming is down to humans – and it's happening faster than normal. Carbon dioxide and methane gases are released into the air as pollution. They are known as greenhouse gases and can stop the Sun's heat escaping from the atmosphere.

▲ Global warming happens when greenhouse gases collect in the Earth's atmosphere. They let heat from the Sun through, but as it bounces back, it gets trapped close to the Earth, making the planet heat up.

Global warming tells us that the climate is changing. Weather changes every day – we have hot days and cold days – but on average the climate is warming up. Scientists think that average temperatures have risen by one degree Celsius in the last 100 years, and that they will keep rising.

I DON'T BELIEVE IT!

Scientists think that sea levels could rise by one metre by 2100 – maybe even more. Three million years ago when the Earth was hotter, the sea was 200 metres higher than today. We could be heading that way again.

Warmer temperatures mean wilder weather. Wind happens when air is heated and gets lighter. It rises up and cold air is sucked in to replace it. Rain occurs when heat makes water in rivers and seas turn into vapour in the air. It rises up and forms rain clouds. Warmer temperatures mean more wind, rain and storms.

KEY

Average area of sea covered by ice from 1980–2000

Predicted area of sea covered by ice for 2080–2100

ARCTIC OCEAN

◄ The ice in the Arctic Ocean is melting so fast that scientists think over half of it could be gone by 2100.

▼ Huge chunks of ice often break off into the sea at Paradise Bay, at the Antarctic.

As the Earth heats up, its ice melts. Vast areas of the Earth are covered in ice. It is found around the North and South Poles, and on high mountains. Now, because of global warming, more and more of this ice is melting. It turns into water and flows into the sea. Also, as the water gets warmer, it expands (gets bigger) and the sea takes up more space, making sea levels rise.

► Polar bears depend on large chunks of ice to hunt and rest on. Melting ice in the Arctic is making life much harder for them.

Energy crisis

We pump greenhouse gases into the atmosphere because we burn fuels to make energy. Cars, planes and trains run on fuel, and we also burn it in power stations to produce electricity. The main fuels – coal, oil and gas – are called fossil fuels because they formed underground over millions of years.

▶ Oil and natural gas formed from the remains of tiny prehistoric sea creatures that collected on the seabed. Layers of rock built up on top and squashed them. Over time, they became underground stores of oil, with pockets of gas above.

Fossil fuels are running out. Because they take so long to form, we are using up fossil fuels much faster than they can be replaced. Eventually, they will become so rare that it will be too expensive to find them. Experts think this will happen before the end of the 21st century.

Oil platform drilling for oil and gas

Hard rock layer

Gas

Oil

Oil and gas move upwards through soft rock layers until reaching a hard rock layer

The layer of dead sea creatures is crushed by rock that forms above, and turns into oil and gas

Tiny sea creatures die and sink to the seabed

QUIZ

Which of these things are used to supply electricity?
A. Burning coal B. Wind
C. The flow of rivers
D. Hamsters on wheels E. Sunshine
F. The energy of earthquakes

Answers:
A, B, C and E. Hamsters could turn tiny turbines, but would make very little electricity. Earthquakes contain vast amounts of energy, but we have not found a way to harness it.

One thing we can do is find other fuels. Besides fossil fuels, we can burn fuels that come from plants. For example, the rape plant contains oil that can be burned in vehicle engines. However, burning these fuels still releases greenhouse gases.

Nuclear power is another kind of energy. By splitting apart atoms – the tiny units that all materials are made of – energy is released, which can be turned into electricity. However, producing this energy creates toxic waste that can make people ill, and may be accidentally released into the air. Safer ways to use nuclear power are being researched.

▲ The Grand Coulee Dam in Washington, USA, holds back a river, creating a lake, or reservoir. Water is let through the dam to turn turbines, which create electricity.

Lots of energy is produced without burning anything. Hydroelectric power stations use the pushing power of flowing rivers to turn turbines. Hydroelectricity is a renewable, or green, energy source – it doesn't use anything up or cause pollution. Scientists are also working on ways to turn the movement of waves and tides into usable energy.

The wind and the Sun are great renewable sources of energy, too. Wind turbines turn generators, which convert the 'turning movement' into electricity. Solar panels work by collecting sunlight and turning it into an electrical current.

◀ Solar panels are made of materials that soak up sunlight and turn its energy into a flow of electricity.

Rotor blade

▲ Modern wind turbines usually have three blades, which spin around at speed in high winds.

13

On the move

Cars release a lot of greenhouse gases. No one had a car 200 years ago. Now, there are around 500 million cars in the world and most are used daily. Cars burn petrol or diesel, which are made from oil – a fossil fuel. We can reduce greenhouse gases and slow down global warming by using cars less.

Carbon dioxide (CO_2)

Nitrogen dioxide (NO_2)

Sulphur dioxide (SO_2)

▲ Car exhaust fumes contain harmful, polluting gases, including sulphur dioxide, nitrogen dioxide and carbon dioxide, which are poisonous to humans.

Public transport is made up of buses, trams and trains that everyone can use. It's a greener way to travel than by car. Buses can carry 60 or 70 people at once and trains can carry several hundred. They still burn fuel, but release much less greenhouse gases per person.

▼ In many cities, there are so many cars that they cause big traffic jams. They move slowly with their engines running, churning out even more pollution.

COUNT YOUR STEPS

Besides saving on greenhouse gases, walking is great exercise and helps you stay healthy. Try counting your steps for one whole day. How many can you do – 3000, 5000 or even 10,000?

Planes fly long distances at high speeds, giving out tonnes of greenhouse gases on each journey. A return flight from the UK to the USA releases more carbon dioxide than a car does in one year. Where you can, travel by boat or train for shorter jouneys.

▶ Maglev trains use magnets to hover above the rails. The magnetic force propels the train forward, rather than a petrol- or diesel-burning engine.

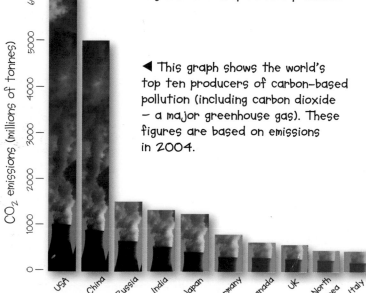

▲ Cyclists in Beijing, China, enjoy World Car-Free Day. This was organized to help reduce pollution.

◀ This graph shows the world's top ten producers of carbon-based pollution (including carbon dioxide – a major greenhouse gas). These figures are based on emissions in 2004.

CO_2 emissions (millions of tonnes)

6000
5000
4000
3000
2000
1000
0

USA, China, Russia, India, Japan, Germany, Canada, UK, North Korea, Italy

The greenest way to get around is to walk. For short journeys, walk instead of going by car. Inside buildings, use the stairs instead of taking lifts and escalators. Cycling is good, too. A bicycle doesn't burn any fuels, it just uses the power of your legs.

Long ago, before engines and turbines were invented, transport worked differently. Boats had sails or oars and were driven by wind or human power, and carts and carriages were pulled by animals. As fossil fuels run out, we may see some old means of transport coming back.

Save energy at home

Saving electricity at home reduces pollution. Most electricity we use is produced from burning fossil fuels. By using less of it, we can cut greenhouse gas emissions. Always turn off lights, TVs, computers and other electrical devices when not in use. Low-energy light bulbs are a good idea, too. They use less power and last longer.

▼ Washing hung outside dries in the heat of the Sun. This saves on electricity and fossil fuels.

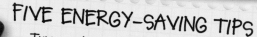

FIVE ENERGY-SAVING TIPS

Turn appliances off properly
Switch appliances off at the 'off' switch or at the plug. Appliances left in standby mode still use electricity.

Make sure your cooking pots have lids on
This saves energy by reducing cooking time.

Don't overfill your kettle
Just boil the amount of water that you need – this will save energy.

Buy fresh foods instead of frozen
Much more energy is used to produce frozen foods, so buy fresh when you can.

Turn down your heating by one degree
You won't really notice the difference, and you could save around 10 percent off your energy bill.

We invent all kinds of electrical gadgets to do things for us, but do we really need them? You can save energy by sweeping the floor instead of using a vacuum cleaner every time. Use your hands to make bread, instead of a food processor. Avoid electrical can openers, knives and other power-hungry gadgets.

Your washing can be green as well as clean! Tumble dryers dry quickly, but they use lots of electricity. In summer, peg your clothes out on a washing line in the garden. In winter, hang them on a drier close to a radiator. You can save even more energy by washing clothes at a lower temperature, such as 30°C.

I DON'T BELIEVE IT!

Only 10 percent of the electricity used by an old-style light bulb is turned into light. The rest turns into wasted heat, which also makes it burn out quicker.

Solar panels are a green way to power a home. They work the same way that solar-powered calculators do – they can change sunlight into electricity straight away. If a home produces more electricity than it needs, it can sell some back to the local energy provider.

▼ Solar panels are often made of silicon. When sunlight hits the silicon, electrical charges can flow as an electrical current.

Sunlight

Sunlight

▲ Solar panels can be installed on rooftops to provide power for homes.

▼ Growing turf on the roof is a good way to insulate a house to prevent heat from escaping and being wasted. The grass uses up CO_2, and makes oxygen, too.

Wires carry the flow of electricity to appliances, such as lights

Solar panel

Turn down the heating in your house and keep warm in other ways! If you're cold put on an extra sweater, or wrap up warm under a cosy blanket or duvet. You will also save energy if your home has insulation in the walls and roof, and double-glazed windows.

Green shopping

Most people buy something from a shop every day. Items such as food, clothes and furniture take a lot of energy to grow, manufacture and then transport to the shops. By doing some smart shopping, you can save some of that energy.

▲ Old plastic bags fill up landfill sites and take hundreds of years to rot away. They can also harm wildlife.

► Bags made from cloth can be used over and over again.

QUIZ

1. Which kind of shopping bag is greenest – plastic, paper or cloth?
2. Which costs more – a litre of bottled water or a litre of tap water?
3. What is vintage clothing?

Answers:
1. A re-usable cloth bag.
2. A litre of bottled water costs up to 1000 times more than tap water.
3. Second-hand clothes.

Say no to plastic bags! Plastic bags are made from oil – a fossil fuel – and it takes energy to make them. However, we often use them once then throw them away, which creates litter and pollution. When you go shopping take a re-usable bag made from cloth, or re-use old plastic bags so that you don't have to use new ones.

How far has your food travelled? The distance food has been transported is called 'food miles'. You can reduce food miles by shopping at farm shops and local markets. In supermarkets, look at packages to find food that was produced nearby. Food that has travelled far is greener if it came by boat, and not by plane.

▶ On the island of Saint Vincent in the Caribbean, people buy bananas that have been grown locally. Bananas grown here are also shipped to other countries – a much greener way to transport than by plane.

More and more people are buying bottled water. Water is heavy and a lot of fuel is needed to transport it long distances. The plastic bottles create waste and cause pollution, too. It's greener to use clean, pure water from the tap at home.

▼ This paper shows that anything can be recycled! Roo Poo paper is made from 80 percent recycled paper and 20 percent kangaroo droppings.

GENUINE ROO POO PAPER

Buying second-hand goods is a great way to save energy. When you buy second-hand clothes, furniture or books nothing new has to be made in a factory. Antique furniture and vintage clothes are often better quality than new things and more individual, too.

Reduce, re-use, recycle

Most of us buy more than we need. We want the latest clothes, toys and cars even though we may not need them – this is called consumerism. Reduce, re-use and recycle is a good way to remember what we can do to reduce the amount of things we buy.

To start with, reduce your shopping. Do you or your family ever buy things that don't end up getting used? Next time, think before you buy – be sure that you are going to use it. Buying less means less things have to be made, transported and thrown away. It saves money, too!

▶ Recycling materials greatly reduces the amount of energy needed to make new products. This graph shows how much energy is saved in making new products using recycled materials, rather than raw materials.

① Empty glass bottles go into a recycling bin

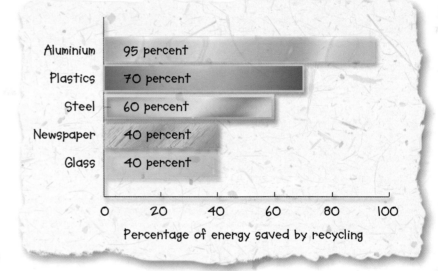

Aluminium	95 percent
Plastics	70 percent
Steel	60 percent
Newspaper	40 percent
Glass	40 percent

0   20   40   60   80   100

Percentage of energy saved by recycling

Recycling means that materials can be made into new things instead of thrown away. This saves energy and makes less waste. Paper, cardboard, food cans, glass and some plastics can all be recycled. Some local councils collect them, or you can take them to a recycling collection point at a school, supermarket or rubbish dump.

② The bottles are collected from the bin and transported to a glass recycling plant

③ The old, broken glass is cleaned and melted down with other substances

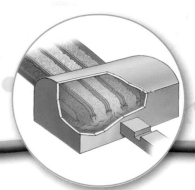

We live in a 'throwaway society'. We are used to disposable things that get used once, then go in the bin. When something breaks, it's easy to get another, but making and transporting these new things uses up raw materials, and creates pollution. Re-use some of the things you throw away – mend clothes by sewing on a new button, pocket or patch and use empty food containers to store things in.

I DON'T BELIEVE IT!

Many things we buy are built to break easily. This is called 'built-in obsolescence'. Manufacturers hope that when your things break, you'll buy new ones from them.

◄ These shopping bags have been made from old, recycled food sacks. They save on raw materials and cut down on plastic bags.

If you can't re-use something yourself, maybe someone else can. Give old clothes, furniture, books and toys to a charity shop, or sell them at a car boot sale or a fundraising jumble sale at school.

6 The bottles are sold and used, and can then be recycled again

▼ Recycled glass is used in road surfaces, concrete production, and a finely ground glass is used to fill golf bunkers. New bottles and jars are also made from recycled glass.

5 The bottles are filled with drinks and labelled

4 The liquid glass is blow moulded (blown with air) into new bottles

Green machines

As well as using machines less, we can use greener ones. Cars, computers and electrical appliances don't have to use lots of energy. Scientists are working on greener versions that use less electricity or fuel – or even none at all.

When hydrogen gas burns, it doesn't release any greenhouse gases – just water. Today, some cars run on hydrogen and create no pollution. However, making the hydrogen for them to run on uses up electricity, and in turn fossil fuels. As fossil fuels run out and renewable energy sources take over, hydrogen cars may become common.

I DON'T BELIEVE IT!

The fastest human-powered vehicles are recumbent cycles, which the rider drives in a lying-down position. They can travel at over 130 kilometres per hour.

▼ A hydrogen-powered car and a hydrogen fuel station show what more of us could be using in the future.

Shell **Hydrogen** Fuel station Vetnisstöö

HYDROGEN3 GM
GM FUEL CELL TECHNOLOGY

HYDROGEN3

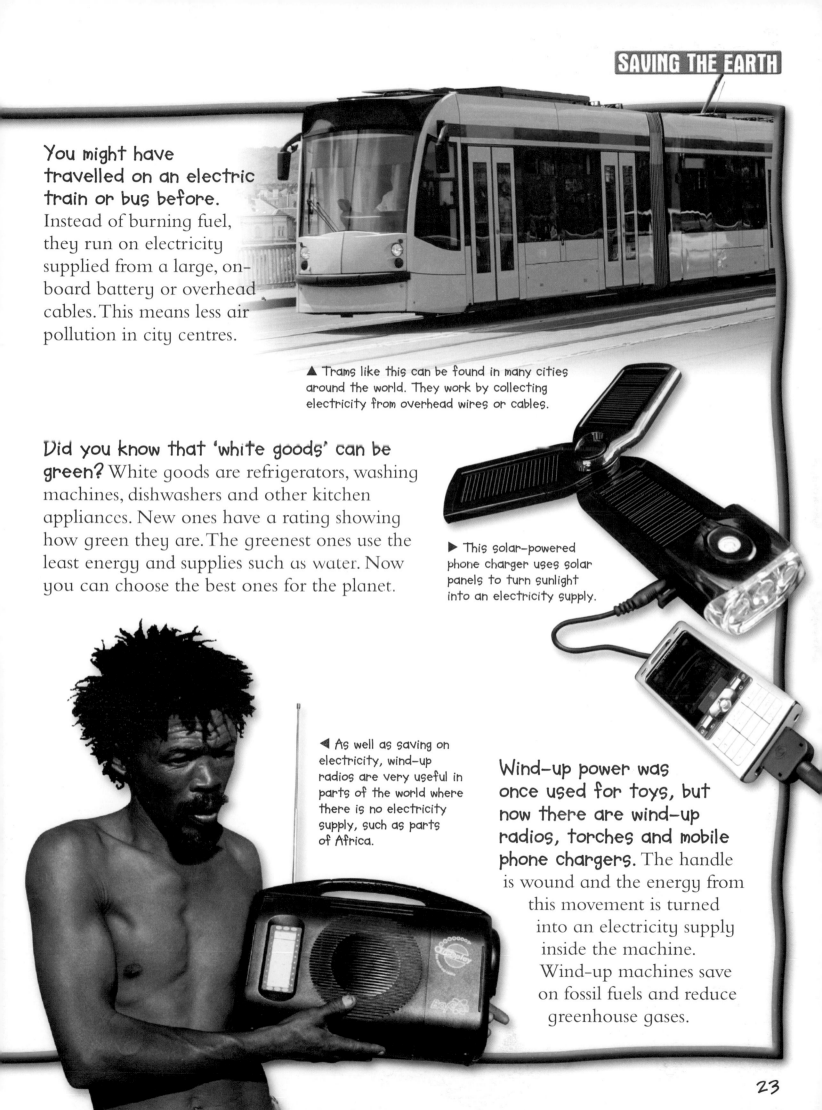

You might have travelled on an electric train or bus before. Instead of burning fuel, they run on electricity supplied from a large, on-board battery or overhead cables. This means less air pollution in city centres.

▲ Trams like this can be found in many cities around the world. They work by collecting electricity from overhead wires or cables.

Did you know that 'white goods' can be green? White goods are refrigerators, washing machines, dishwashers and other kitchen appliances. New ones have a rating showing how green they are. The greenest ones use the least energy and supplies such as water. Now you can choose the best ones for the planet.

► This solar-powered phone charger uses solar panels to turn sunlight into an electricity supply.

◄ As well as saving on electricity, wind-up radios are very useful in parts of the world where there is no electricity supply, such as parts of Africa.

Wind-up power was once used for toys, but now there are wind-up radios, torches and mobile phone chargers. The handle is wound and the energy from this movement is turned into an electricity supply inside the machine. Wind-up machines save on fossil fuels and reduce greenhouse gases.

23

Science solutions

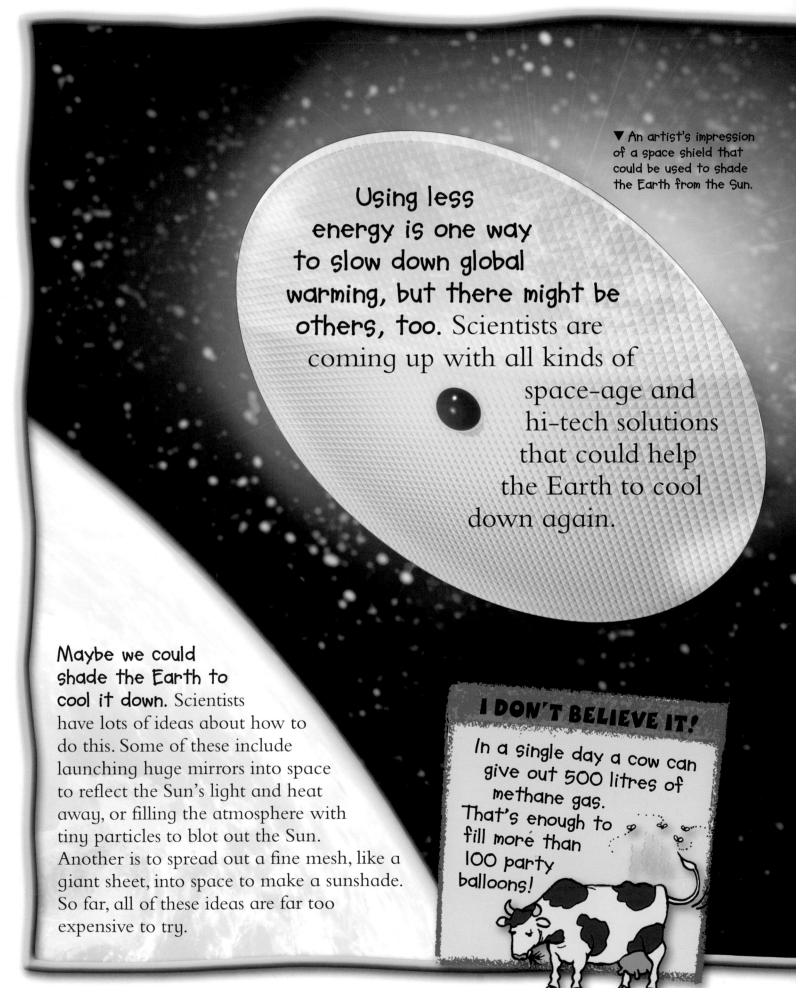

▼ An artist's impression of a space shield that could be used to shade the Earth from the Sun.

Using less energy is one way to slow down global warming, but there might be others, too. Scientists are coming up with all kinds of space-age and hi-tech solutions that could help the Earth to cool down again.

Maybe we could shade the Earth to cool it down. Scientists have lots of ideas about how to do this. Some of these include launching huge mirrors into space to reflect the Sun's light and heat away, or filling the atmosphere with tiny particles to blot out the Sun. Another is to spread out a fine mesh, like a giant sheet, into space to make a sunshade. So far, all of these ideas are far too expensive to try.

I DON'T BELIEVE IT!

In a single day a cow can give out 500 litres of methane gas. That's enough to fill more than 100 party balloons!

▶ A huge cloud of green algae can be seen near the shore of Lake Tahoe, USA. Algae is made up of millions of tiny plants. There is so much algae in the world that it soaks up a lot of the world's carbon dioxide.

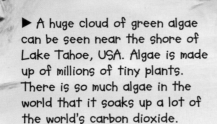

Instead of greenhouse gases filling the air, we could soak them up. Plants naturally take in carbon dioxide (CO_2) – a greenhouse gas – so planting lots of trees helps to slow global warming. Scientists are also trying to develop special types of algae (tiny plants) that can soak up even more greenhouse gases.

Sunlight

Sugars (food for the plant)

Water

CO_2

Oxygen

▲ Plants make food using sunlight, by a process called photosynthesis. They use up carbon dioxide and give out oxygen.

We could catch greenhouse gases before they escape into the air. There are already devices that can do this, which capture carbon dioxide from power stations and factory chimneys. Once it is caught, the gas needs to be stored safely. Scientists are looking at ways of storing carbon dioxide, or changing it into something harmless.

▼ A special foam wrapping is unrolled over the Tortin glacier in Switzerland to stop it melting.

As they digest grass, cows and other grazing animals pass a lot of wind! This gas contains methane – a greenhouse gas. Besides burning fuels, this is one of the biggest causes of global warming. Scientists are experimenting with feeding cows different foods to reduce the amount of methane.

Pollution problems

Pollution means dirt, waste and other substances that damage our surroundings. Our farms and factories often release harmful chemicals into rivers and lakes, and cars, lorries and other road vehicles give out poisonous, polluting gases. Litter and rubbish are pollution, too.

▼ A thick layer of smog hangs over the city of Bangkok, the capital of Thailand.

Humans make waste — when we go to the toilet. The waste and water from our toilets is called sewage. This usually ends up at sewage works where we process it to make it safe, but in some places sewage flows straight into rivers or the sea. It is smelly and dirty and can contain deadly germs.

Pollution can harm our health. Smog is a mixture of smoke from factories and motor vehicles, and fog, and it collects over some cities. It makes it harder to breathe, worsening illnesses such as asthma.

◄ People in Kuala Lumpur, the capital of Malaysia, wear masks to avoid breathing in smog.

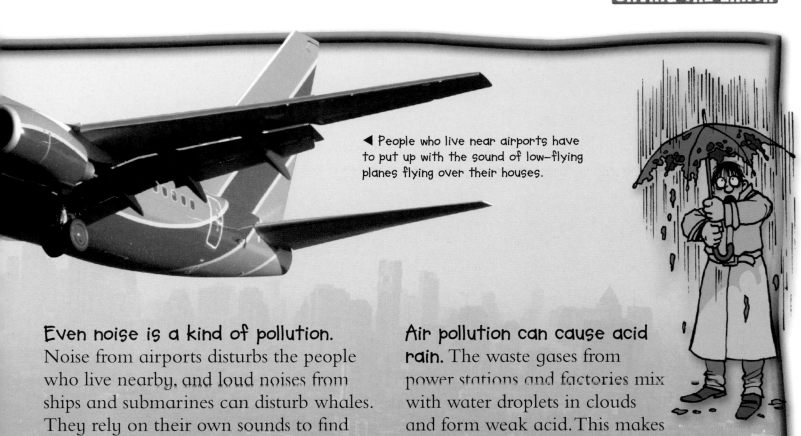

◀ People who live near airports have to put up with the sound of low-flying planes flying over their houses.

Even noise is a kind of pollution. Noise from airports disturbs the people who live nearby, and loud noises from ships and submarines can disturb whales. They rely on their own sounds to find their way and send messages, so other noises can confuse them.

Air pollution can cause acid rain. The waste gases from power stations and factories mix with water droplets in clouds and form weak acid. This makes soil, rivers and lakes more acidic, which can kill fish and plants. Acid rain can even make rock crumble and dissolve.

The more we throw away, the more rubbish piles up. When we drop rubbish just anywhere, it becomes litter. If we put rubbish in the bin, some of it may get recycled, and the rest gets taken away and dumped in a big hole in the ground, called a landfill site. Either way, there's too much of it!

▶ At landfill sites, rubbish piles up making huge mountains of waste that have to be flattened down by rollers.

TRUE OR FALSE?

1. Rubbish isn't a problem if you put it in a bin.
2. Acid rain can make your nose fall off.
3. Loud noises in the ocean can make whales get lost.

Answers:
1. False – it still piles up in landfill sites. 2. False – the acid is not very strong, but it can dissolve away the stone nose of a statue. 3. True – according to some scientists.

Litter and rubbish

After leaving your house, rubbish has a long life ahead of it. Things such as banana skins will rot away quickly, but man-made products such as plastics take a long time to decay and break down. That's why landfill sites fill up fast, and we have to find more and more space for our rubbish.

▶ Forest fires caused by dropped litter, such as glass bottles and cigarette ends, can be deadly and cost a lot of money to put out. Here, a helicopter drops water onto a forest fire.

A drinks bottle left in a dry field or forest could start a fire. The curved glass in a bottle – especially a piece of a broken bottle – can act like a magnifying glass. If it focuses the Sun's heat on a dry patch of grass, a fire can start.

I DON'T BELIEVE IT!

People drop the most litter from cars because they think they can make a quick getaway! However, governments are making new laws to stop littering from cars.

► Leaving your junk in a public place is known as fly-tipping. Mattresses, tyres and shopping trolleys are often dumped in the countryside.

Some people treat the countryside and other public places as a dumping ground. Big items, such as mattresses, sofas and shopping trolleys, are sometimes dumped on roadsides or in rivers. Besides looking a mess, these things can release poisons as they rot away.

The plastic rings that hold cans together can be deadly for wildlife. These stretchy loops are used to hold drinks cans together in packs. As litter, they can get caught around the neck of a wild animal, such as a seagull, and strangle it. Snip the loops open with scissors before throwing them in the bin.

◄ Ducks struggle through a pond polluted with plastic bottles.

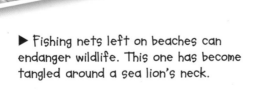

► Fishing nets left on beaches can endanger wildlife. This one has become tangled around a sea lion's neck.

Fishing weights and lines left near rivers and lakes can choke or strangle water wildlife. Weights sometimes contain lead and this can poison water birds, such as swans. People who go fishing should make sure they never leave any of their equipment behind.

Reducing waste

There are lots of things you can do to reduce waste. When you throw something away, think if it could be recycled or re-used instead. Avoid buying things that will have to be thrown away after one use.

MAKE SOME COMPOST

Make a heap of plant waste, fruit and vegetable skins and grass cuttings in a corner of your garden. It takes a few months to turn into compost. To help it along, mix it around and dig it over with a garden fork. When the compost is ready, you can use it for potting plants or add it to soil in your garden.

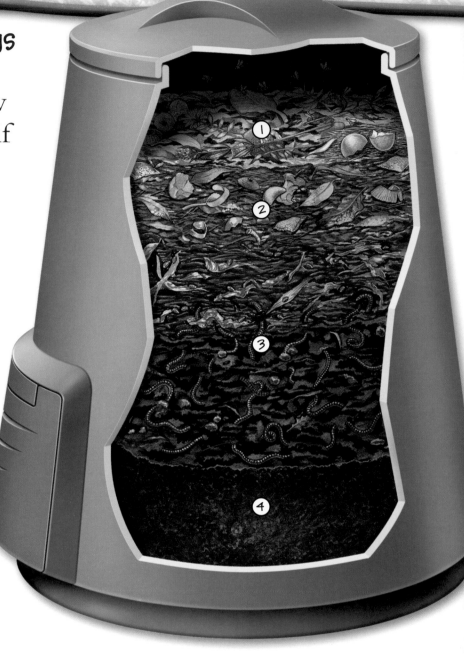

▲ You can buy a specially made compost bin to make compost in, like this one.

Instead of throwing away fruit and vegetable peelings, turn them into compost. When your peelings rot down, they turn into a rich, fertile soil that's great for your garden. All you need is a space outside where you can pile up your waste for composting, or you can get a special compost bin.

The composting process

1. Waste, including fruit and vegetable peelings, tea bags, leaves and eggshells, goes in the top.

2. Tiny organisms called microbes start to break down the waste, which makes it heat up.

3. Insects help to break it down even more and worms help air to get into the compost.

4. The compost is brown and moist and should smell earthy.

Millions of disposable batteries end up in landfill sites every year. They take a long time to decay and when they do, they release harmful chemicals. Rechargeable batteries can be refilled with energy from the mains and re-used many times.

Reduce your waste – pick re-usables, not disposables. Face wipes and disposable nappies, cups and cooking trays are all things that we use once, then throw away. It's greener to use re-useables, such as washable baking trays, cloth tea towels and washable nappies.

Lots of the things we buy come wrapped up several times over. We take them home, unwrap them and throw the packaging away. Choose products with less packaging, or none at all.

▼ Much of our rubbish is made up of pointless packaging that we don't really need.

TIME TO DECOMPOSE

Fruit and vegetables	2 days to 6 months
Newspaper	6 months
Drinks cans	100 to 500 years
Disposable nappies	200 to 500 years
Plastic bags	450 years
Plastic bottles	100 to 1000 years +

WASTE SYSTEMS

Cutting pollution

Big companies need to cut the pollution they produce. There are laws to ban them dumping toxic chemicals and to limit dangerous waste gases, but they're not yet tough enough to make a big difference. Pressure groups such as Greenpeace are fighting for stronger, better laws.

▲ This tractor is spraying chemicals onto crops to kill pests and weeds. When it rains the chemicals wash into rivers and can harm wildlife.

Weedkillers and insect sprays kill unwanted plants and bugs in the garden. However, because they are poisonous they can kill other wildlife too, and cause pollution. It's greener to pull up weeds and pick off pests instead.

► This tractor is using a different method — cutting back weeds between the crops, instead of spraying them. This keeps the environment cleaner.

Cleaning your house can make the planet dirty! Strong cleaning chemicals that are washed down the sink can end up in water supplies. Try to use less of them, or use natural, home-made alternatives. A mixture of water and vinegar is great for cleaning windows.

▶ Some companies are now making re-useable washing balls that clean clothes without using any detergent.

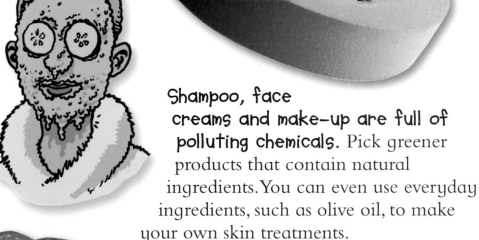

Paint, paint stripper and varnish contain toxic chemicals. These chemicals don't break down naturally when they are poured away, which results in pollution. If you can, save them to use again, or see if your local council will collect them for re-using (some councils do this).

Shampoo, face creams and make-up are full of polluting chemicals. Pick greener products that contain natural ingredients. You can even use everyday ingredients, such as olive oil, to make your own skin treatments.

▲ Soap nuts are berries of the soapberry tree. They contain a natural, soapy chemical that can be used to wash clothes.

MAKE A FOOT SOAK

Mix together:
1 tablespoon of fine oatmeal
1 tablespoon of skimmed milk powder
1 teaspoonful of dried rosemary

Spoon the mixture into an old, clean sock and tie a knot at the top. Leave the sock in a bowl of warm water for a few minutes, then soak your feet in the water for 20 minutes.

Wildlife in danger

▲ Wild animals, such as leopards and tigers, are still killed for their fur to make items such as handbags and rugs.

Since humans have existed on Earth, many living things have been destroyed. To make space for cities, farms and roads, people have taken over wild areas, and plants and animals have lost their natural homes, or habitats. This is called habitat loss and it is the main reason why wildlife is in danger.

Toxic waste, oil spills and pesticides can be deadly for wildlife. In the 1950s, a chemical called DDT was used to kill insects on crops, but it affected other animals including wild birds. It made them lay eggs with very thin shells that cracked easily. The birds began to die out as they could not have chicks.

▼ This bird is covered in oil spilt from an oil tanker (a ship that carries oil). If birds like this aren't cleaned, they will die.

▲ These nature reserve wardens in Dzanga-Ndoki National Park in the Central African Republic have caught some poachers hunting protected animals.

Wild plants and animals suffer when we exploit them — use them to meet our needs. Humans hunt wild animals for their skins, meat and other body parts, such as ivory from elephants' tusks. Some people steal wild plants, too. If too many are taken, their numbers fall fast.

QUIZ

What do these words mean?
1. Extinct 2. Species
3. Endangered 4. Habitat

Answers:
1. Died out and no longer existing. 2. A particular type of living thing. 3. In danger of becoming extinct. 4. The surroundings where a plant or animal lives.

Human activities have wiped out some species, or types, of living things. When a species no longer exists, it is said to be extinct. The great auk — a large-beaked, black-and-white sea bird — became extinct in the 1850s due to hunting by humans. Many other species are now close to extinction, including the tiger and mountain gorilla.

▼ The orang-utan – a type of ape – is an extremely threatened species, and one of our closest animal cousins.

When a creature is in danger of becoming extinct, we call it threatened. Severely threatened species are known as endangered. These labels help to teach people about the dangers to wildlife. They also help us to make laws to try to protect these species from hunters and collectors.

35

Saving habitats

To save wildlife, we need to save habitats. Humans are taking up more and more space and if we don't slow down, there'll be no wild, natural land left. We need to leave plenty of natural areas for wildlife to live in.

▲ These penguins live in Antarctica. Their habitat is ice and freezing water and it could be affected by global warming.

One hundred years ago, people went on safari to hunt animals. Today, more tourists go to watch wild animals and plants in their natural habitat – this is called ecotourism and it helps wildlife. Local people can make enough money from tourism, so they don't need to hunt. However, ecotourism can disturb wildlife, so tourists have to take care where they go.

Nature reserves and national parks are safe homes for wildlife. The land is kept wild and unspoiled to preserve natural habitats. There are also guards or wardens to protect the wildlife and watch out for hunters.

▶ Tourists in a jeep approach a pride of lions in a nature reserve in South Africa.

▲ As the human population continues to rise, more and more wild, natural land is being taken over.

It can be hard for humans to preserve habitats because we need space too. There are nearly 7 billion (7,000,000,000) humans on Earth today. Experts think this will rise to at least 9 billion. Some countries have laws to limit the number of children people are allowed to have to try to control the population.

▼ A diver explores a coral reef. The corals are home to many species of fish, crabs and shellfish.

You can help to keep habitats safe. In the countryside, don't take stones, shells or flowers. Visit nature reserves — your money helps to run them. Don't buy souvenirs made of coral, or other animals or plants, as this encourages hunting and habitat destruction.

I DON'T BELIEVE IT!

The river Thames in London has just 10 percent of the pollution it had in the 1950s because of pollution prevention, and is home to over 100 species of fish.

In the garden

If you have a garden at home or at school, you could make it into a safe place for wildlife to live. Gardens are parts of towns and cities that can stay wild. They can be a good habitat for many species of small animals and wild plants.

◀ An insect box provides a home for creatures, such as bees and ladybirds.

▼ Hedgehogs like hiding under leaves. If you have hedgehogs in your garden, don't give them milk as it's bad for them, but try meat scraps, berries and grated cheese instead.

Wild creatures love a messy garden. If gardens are always tidy there is nowhere for animals to hide. Leave parts of your garden untidy and overgrown – let grass and weeds grow and don't clear up piles of leaves. These areas provide shelter and homes for spiders, beetles, birds and hedgehogs.

FOOD FOR BIRDS

Here are some snacks to try putting out for garden birds:
Grated hard cheese
Raisins
Sunflower seeds or other seeds
Chopped or crushed nuts
Meat scraps
Fresh, chopped coconut

Avoid putting out dry or salty food, such as stale bread or salted nuts, as it's bad for birds.

You can help wild birds by feeding them. Feed birds in winter – there are fewer berries and insects for them to eat at this time of year. Put up a bird table, or hang bird feeders from trees in your garden.

▲ Butterflies such as tortoiseshells like to feed on the flowers of a buddleia bush.

◄ A coal tit and a red squirrel are helping themselves to nuts from this bird feeder.

Bees and butterflies feed on nectar – a sweet juice found inside flowers. A garden full of flowers will provide lots of food for insects. They especially like sunflowers, lavender and buddleia bushes.

▶ Sunflowers are great for wildlife. They provide nectar for insects and nutritious seeds for birds.

Thick, thorny bushes are brilliant for birds. Some bushes, such as brambles and hawthorns, provide berries that birds like to eat. Thick, tangled bushes also make safe places for birds to build their nests or hide from animals, such as pet cats.

39

Saving species

Goods made from threatened wildlife species can be bought around the world. Although there are laws to protect plants and animals, they are often broken. It's best not to buy anything that might come from a threatened species, such as ivory, skins, horns or bones.

◄ Parrots are sometimes stolen from the wild as chicks and sold as pets.

Exotic pets can be exciting, but they are sometimes stolen from the wild. Avoid having an unusual pet such as a rare lizard or parrot. It could be a threatened species that has been taken away from its natural habitat.

You or your class could sponsor an endangered animal, such as a tiger. You pay a small fee that goes towards caring for the animal and running the zoo or reserve where it lives. In return, you'll get letters or emails about your animal's progress. Zoos and wildlife organizations can help you to do this.

◀ A Greenpeace ship (far left) encounters a whaling ship, the Nisshin Maru, in the Antarctic Ocean. Some countries still hunt whales, but campaigning groups such as Greenpeace are trying to stop it.

I DON'T BELIEVE IT!

Millions of sharks, including threatened species, are hunted every year to make shark's fin soup. The soup is an expensive delicacy in China.

People still hunt threatened species, even though it's illegal. Many people in the world are very poor and some can't resist hunting a threatened tiger to sell its skin, or a shark to sell its fins. Governments need to try to reduce poverty, to help wildlife as well as people.

▼ In China, giant pandas are being bred successfully on wildlife reserves. These are just some of the new babies born in recent years.

To help endangered animals, visit your nearest zoo. Most zoos have captive breeding programmes. These help endangered animals to have babies to increase their numbers. Some can then be released back into the wild.

41

Forests and farms

Every year, over 12 million hectares of forests are logged (cut down). That's an area the size of the country of Malawi in Africa, or the US state of Pennsylvania. Trees do grow again, but we are cutting forests down much faster than they can grow back.

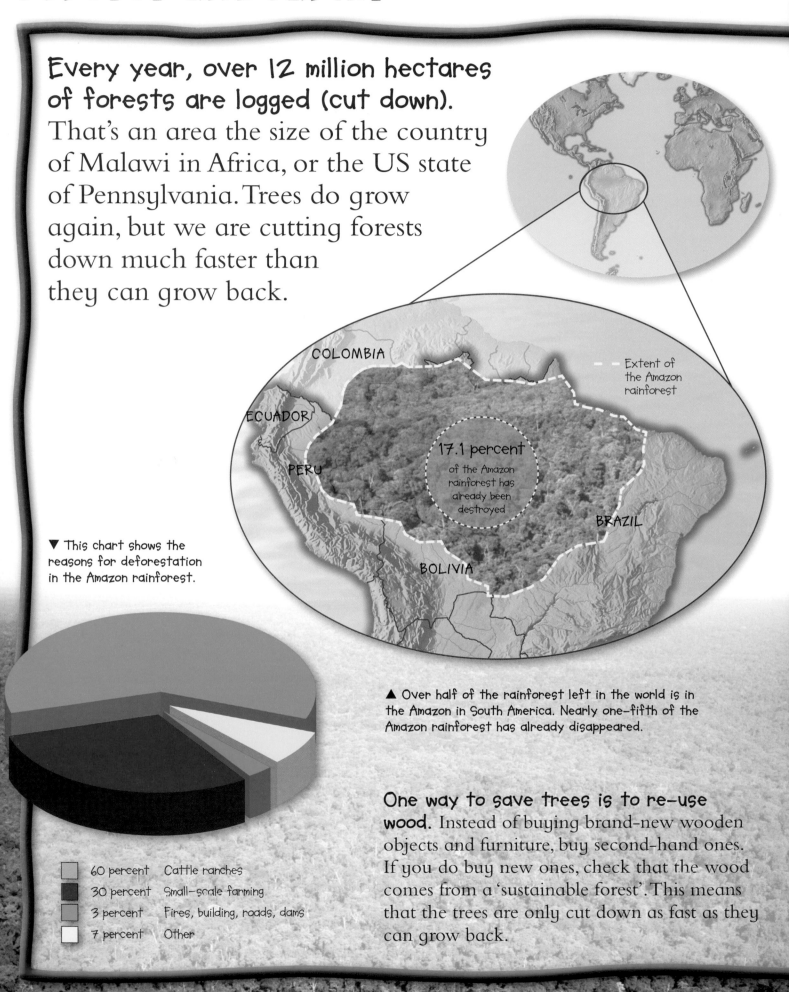

COLOMBIA

ECUADOR

PERU

BOLIVIA

BRAZIL

- - - Extent of the Amazon rainforest

17.1 percent of the Amazon rainforest has already been destroyed

▼ This chart shows the reasons for deforestation in the Amazon rainforest.

▲ Over half of the rainforest left in the world is in the Amazon in South America. Nearly one-fifth of the Amazon rainforest has already disappeared.

	60 percent	Cattle ranches
	30 percent	Small-scale farming
	3 percent	Fires, building, roads, dams
	7 percent	Other

One way to save trees is to re-use wood. Instead of buying brand-new wooden objects and furniture, buy second-hand ones. If you do buy new ones, check that the wood comes from a 'sustainable forest'. This means that the trees are only cut down as fast as they can grow back.

Farms take up almost 40 percent of the Earth's land. We need farms to provide us with food – to grow crops and keep animals on – but they have a big impact on the Earth. Most farmland is devoted to one type of crop or animal, so many types of wildlife that live there lose their homes.

▲ Large areas of rainforest in Indonesia and Malaysia have been cut down to make way for oil palm tree plantations. The fruits of the oil palm are harvested for their oil, which can be found in one in ten supermarket products.

Organic farming can be a greener way to farm. It doesn't use artificial chemicals, such as pesticides and fertilizers, which means it is good for wildlife and the soil. If you buy organic food and other products, you help to keep the Earth cleaner.

I DON'T BELIEVE IT!

In prehistoric times, forests covered more than half of the Earth's land. Today, almost half of those forests have gone.

▶ As most nuts grow on trees, they are one crop that can be grown without cutting them down.

Buying nuts can help save the rainforests. Some products, such as brazil nuts, grow on rainforest trees. By buying them, you are helping farmers to keep rainforests alive, instead of cutting them down to grow other crops.

Seas and coasts

Seas and oceans cover the biggest part of the Earth's surface – nearly three-quarters of it! Pollution, global warming and fishing have a huge effect on the sea and its wildlife.

Pollution from farms, factories and houses often flows into rivers and ends up in the sea. Tiny sea plants and animals absorb the chemicals. When they are eaten by larger sea creatures, the polluting chemicals are passed on from one animal to the next. Many large sea creatures, such as sharks and polar bears, have been found to have a lot of toxic chemicals in their bodies.

Coastal areas are in trouble because of rising sea levels. As the sea rises, tides, tsunamis and storm waves can reach further inland. If the sea rises much more, it could put many coastal cities underwater. The danger of the sea flooding the land is one of the biggest reasons to try to slow global warming down.

◄ In Thailand, signs on beaches and streets give warnings and provide evacuation directions to be used in the event of a tsunami. Thailand is one of the countries that was devastated by the tsunami that struck on December 26, 2004.

For thousands of years, humans have hunted fish. Today, we are catching so many fish that some types are in danger of disappearing – this is called overfishing. To try to stop it, there are laws to give fishing boats a quota, or limit, on how many fish they can catch.

▼ Low-lying islands, such as this one in Fiji, are in danger of disappearing as sea levels rise.

▶ Cod is one type of fish that has been overfished in some parts of the world.

There's precious treasure in the seabed. It contains oil – a fossil fuel – and many other useful minerals. However, drilling and digging into the seabed damages wildlife and sea habitats, such as coral reefs.

Governments are starting to set up nature reserves in the sea, as well as on land. In these areas, no mining or drilling is allowed.

◀ Oil rigs such as this one are built around a giant drill that bores into the seabed to extract oil.

Water resources

The world is using too much water. In many places, water is being pumped out of lakes, rivers and underground wells faster than rain can replace it. As the human population grows, so will the need for water.

▼ Most of the world's freshwater is frozen! The figures below show where the fresh water is found.

Ice caps and glaciers
77.2 percent

Ground water
22.26 percent

Rivers and lakes
0.32 percent

Soil
0.18 percent

Atmosphere
0.04 percent

Global warming is causing huge water problems. Some areas are getting more rain and floods, as hotter temperatures lead to more clouds and storms. Floods often pollute water supplies. Other places are becoming hotter and drier, leading to droughts. Either way, global warming is leading to water shortages.

▼ This boat was left high and dry in the Aral Sea in central Asia, which is shrinking because its water has been drained to water crops.

▶ Villagers in Pakistan collect water from a deep well after a rain shower during a drought.

In some countries, drinking water comes from the sea. Seawater is much too salty to drink, but in dry countries, such as Kuwait, they have factories called desalination plants. They take the salt out of seawater to make it fit to drink. However this process uses up lots of energy and is not a long-term solution.

Having a green garden saves water! Many people pave their gardens over for a patio, but rain flows straight off the hard surface and can lead to floods. If gardens are kept as soil and plants, rain soaks into the ground and keeps water supplies topped up.

▼ An aerial view of a desalination plant in Kuwait.

Seawater enters here and is forced through the filter

Salt molecules cannot pass through the filter

Fine filter

Water molecule

▲ The salt is removed from seawater by pushing it through a very fine filter, making it drinkable. This process is called reverse osmosis.

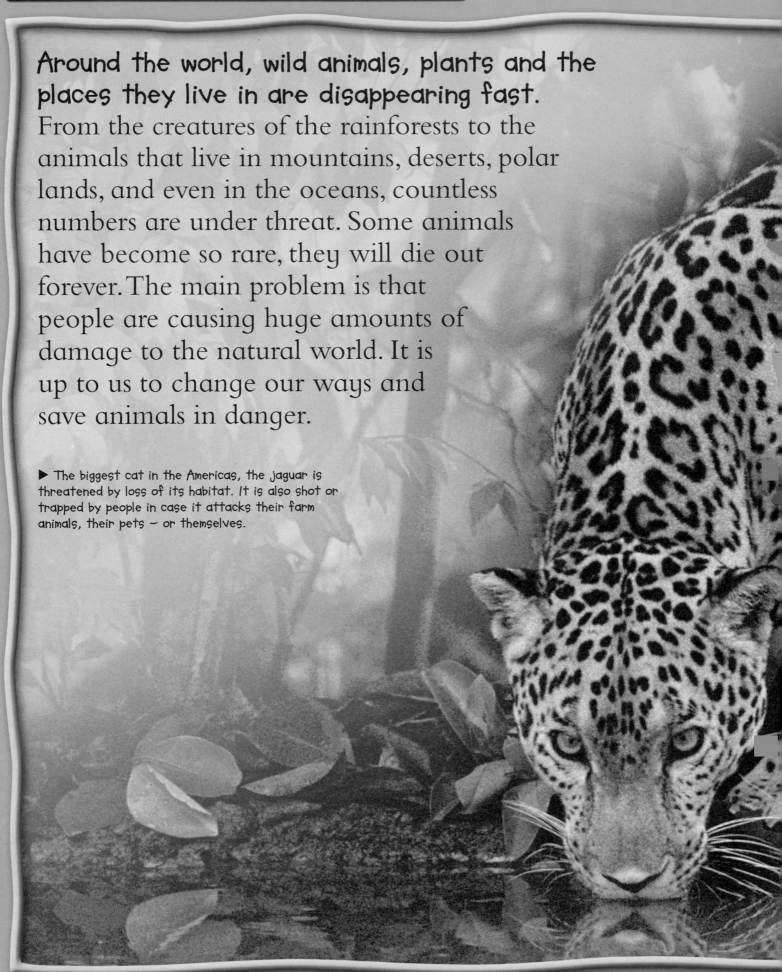

ENDANGERED ANIMALS

Around the world, wild animals, plants and the places they live in are disappearing fast. From the creatures of the rainforests to the animals that live in mountains, deserts, polar lands, and even in the oceans, countless numbers are under threat. Some animals have become so rare, they will die out forever. The main problem is that people are causing huge amounts of damage to the natural world. It is up to us to change our ways and save animals in danger.

▶ The biggest cat in the Americas, the jaguar is threatened by loss of its habitat. It is also shot or trapped by people in case it attacks their farm animals, their pets — or themselves.

Too late to save

In the last few hundred years, many kinds of animals have become endangered, and dozens have died out. They include fish, frogs, snakes, birds and mammals. Studying why these extinctions happened can help to save today's endangered animals.

Being very common is no safeguard against human threats. Five hundred years ago there were perhaps 5000 million passenger pigeons. They were shot and trapped by people for their meat, and their natural habitats were taken over by crops and farm animals. The last passenger pigeon, 'Martha', died in Cincinnati Zoo in 1914.

A creature that went from discovery to extinction in less than 30 years was Steller's sea cow. It was a huge, 3-tonne cousin of the manatee and dugong, and lived in the Arctic region. It was first described by scientists in 1741. So many were killed in a short space of time, that Steller's sea cow had died out by 1768.

QUIZ

What died out when?
Put these animals' extinctions in order, from most long ago to most recent.
A. Dodo
B. Blue antelope
C. Thylacine
D. Passenger pigeon
E. Steller's sea cow

Answers:
A E B D C

▶ The dodo has become a world symbol of extinction. Only a few bones, feathers and bits of skin remain.

▲ Steller's sea cow was 8 metres long and almost as heavy as an elephant. However size was no protection, as its herds were slaughtered by sailors for meat, blubber and hides.

The dodo, a turkey-sized bird with tiny wings that could not fly, was found on the island of Mauritius in the Indian Ocean. Sailors that stopped at the island captured dodos as fresh food. So many were killed that all dodos were extinct by 1700. This has led to the saying 'as dead as a dodo'.

▼ Every 7 September, Australia holds National Threatened Species Day. The day is in memory of the last thylacine that died on this date in 1936 at Hobart Zoo, in the state of Tasmania.

Many animals have become endangered, and died out forever. They include the blue antelope of Southern Africa (around 1800), the flightless seabird known as the great auk (1850s), the dog-like marsupial (pouched mammal) known as the thylacine or Tasmanian tiger (1936), and the Caribbean monk seal (1950s). The list is very long, and very sad.

How we Know

How do we know which animals are endangered and need our help?

Explorers and travellers bring back stories of rare and strange creatures. Sometimes they add bits to their tales to make them more exciting. Scientific studies and surveys are needed to find out which creatures are in trouble, and how serious the threats are.

▼ This lion, put to sleep briefly by a tranquillizer dart, is being tracked by its radio collar. Each lion has its own pattern of whisker spots, like a fingerprint, to help identify it.

▼ Rangers guard incredibly rare mountain gorillas, which soon get used to having them around. The rangers become well acquainted with the habits of the gorillas, which helps scientists carry out important research.

Firing a dart containing a knock-out chemical makes a creature, such as a lion, sleep for a short time. Scientists then work fast to take blood samples, check for diseases, measure and weigh, and gather other useful information, before the animal wakes up.

Scientists need to know more than just how many individual animals are left in an endangered species. They try to find out the animals' ages, what they eat, how often they breed, how they move about or migrate, and how long they live. This all helps to build up knowledge of the species, and work out the best ways to take action.

▼ Aerial films and photographs can be studied to count big animals such as elephants, estimate their age and work out if they are male or female.

Big animals in open habitats, such as elephants on the African savanna (grassland), are surveyed from the air. Planes, helicopters and even balloons carry people who count the herds and take photographs.

I DON'T BELIEVE IT!

When studying an endangered animal, one of the best things to have is — its poo! Droppings or dung contain much information about what a creature eats, how healthy it is, and any diseases it may have.

It is extremely helpful to capture, tag and release animals. Rare birds such as albatrosses are carefully caught in nets, and small rings are put on their legs. This helps scientists to identify each albatross every time it is seen. Tags in the ears of rhinos can work in the same way.

Some animals are big enough to attach a radio beacon to, which sends signals up to a satellite. Whales, sea turtles, seals and other sea creatures can be tracked as they swim across the vast oceans.

How endangered?

We might suspect an animal is at risk, but how serious is the threat? The scientific organization called the IUCN, World Conservation Union, produces a 'Red List' of threatened species of animals and plants. Each species is given a two-letter description to show its plight.

▲ The leafy sea dragon is threatened as it is caught by exotic fish collectors. It is also killed, dried and powdered for the traditional medicine trade.

NT is Near Threatened. A species could be in trouble soon, but not quite yet. An example is the leafy sea dragon, a type of fish, whose flaps of skin make it look like swaying seaweed.

VU is Vulnerable. The species is already under threat, and help is needed over the coming years. An example is the northern fur seal, of the northern Pacific region.

◄ The northern fur seal was killed in large numbers for its thick, soft, warm fur, once used for coats.

► Cheetahs once lived across most of Africa and the Middle East, and were even partly tamed and kept as pets by royalty. They may disappear before long.

EN is Endangered. The species faces big problems and the risk of extinction over the coming years is high. An example is the cheetah, the fastest runner on Earth.

CR is Critically Endangered. This is the most serious group. Unless there is a huge conservation effort, extinction is just around the corner. An example is the vaquita, the smallest kind of porpoise, from the northern Gulf of California.

▲ Polluted water, drilling for oil and gas, and being caught in fishing nets are all deadly dangers for the 1.5-metre-long vaquita.

▼ Hawaiian crows are only found in captivity. Attempts to breed and release them have so far failed.

MATCH UP

Can you place these threatened creatures in their correct animal groups?

A. Whale shark
B. Spix macaw
C. Vaquita
D. Caiman
E. Olm

1. Bird
2. Fish
3. Amphibian
4. Mammal
5. Reptile

Answers:
A2 B1 C4 D5 E3

EW is Extinct in the Wild. The species has disappeared in nature, although there may be a few surviving in zoos and wildlife parks. An example is the Hawaiian crow. The last two wild birds disappeared in 2002, although some live in cages. EX is Extinct, or gone forever. Usually this means the animal has not been seen for 50 years.

On the critical list

The most threatened animals in the world are CR, Critically Endangered. One of the most famous CR mammals is the mountain gorilla. There are just a few hundred left in the high peaks of Central Africa. They suffer from loss of their natural habitat, being killed for meat and trophies, and from catching human diseases.

▲ Smallest of the rhinos, at about 700 kilograms, the Sumatran rhino is poached for its horns. These are powdered for use in traditional so-called 'medicines'.

The most threatened group of big mammals is the rhinos. Of the five species, three are CR – the Javan and Sumatran rhinos of Southeast Asia, and the black rhino of Africa. The Indian rhino is endangered, EN. They all suffer from loss of natural living areas and being killed for their horns.

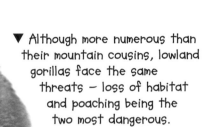

▼ Although more numerous than their mountain cousins, lowland gorillas face the same threats – loss of habitat and poaching being the two most dangerous.

MAKE A RHINO NOSE

You will need:
large sheet of card   sticky tape

A rhino's nose horn may be more than one metre long! Make your own by rolling some card into a cone shape and taping it firmly. Hold the 'horn' angled up from your own nose. How do rhinos see where they are going?

The kouprey or Cambodian forest ox is another critical mammal. It has big horns and weighs more than one tonne, but there are probably fewer than 250 left in Southeast Asia. Apart from losing its natural habitat, the kouprey is hunted by local people and it catches diseases from farm cattle. It is also killed for food by soldiers who fight for local warlords and hide in the forest.

▲ The kouprey grazes on grasses by night and hides in the thick forest during the day.

▼ Right whales are slow swimmers and stay near the surface, which made them easy targets for whalers.

The northern right whale has never recovered from being slaughtered during the mass killing of whales in the last century. There are now probably less than 600 left. These whales breed so slowly that they may never increase in numbers.

Apart from big, well-known mammals, many other smaller mammal species are on the critical list. They include the hispid hare (Assam rabbit) and dwarf blue sheep of the Himalaya Mountains, and the northern hairy-nosed wombat of northeast Australia.

All kinds under threat

Mammals such as pandas, whales and tigers are not the only endangered animals – there are many other threatened species from all animal groups.

Among the birds is the Bermuda petrel, the national seabird of the island of Bermuda. Only about 250 survive and the islanders are making a huge conservation effort to help them.

◄ The young Bermuda petrel stays at sea for about five years before it comes back to land to breed.

A critical reptile is the Batagur baska (river turtle or terrapin) of India and Southeast Asia. One reason for its rarity was that people collected its eggs, especially in Cambodia, to give as presents to the king. King Norodom Sihamoni of Cambodia has now given orders to protect the baska.

▶ The batagur 'royal turtle' grows to more than one metre long and 30 kilograms in weight. It eats all kinds of foods, from plants to fish and crabs.

An endangered amphibian is Hamilton's frog of New Zealand. It is perhaps the rarest frog in the world. Hamilton's frog does not croak, does not have webbed feet, and hatches from its egg not as a tadpole, but as a fully formed froglet.

▼ The Devil's Hole pupfish is one of several very rare fish, each found in one small pool.

▲ Hamilton's frog is less than 5 cm long. There may be as few as 300 left in the wild.

A fish that is vulnerable (VU) is the Devil's Hole pupfish. It lives naturally in just one warm pool, Devil's Hole, in a limestone cave in the desert near Death Valley, USA. There are usually around 200–400 pupfish there, but after problems with floods and droughts, the number by 2006 was less than 50.

One of the rarest insects is the Queen Alexandra's birdwing butterfly. It lives in a small area on the island of Papua New Guinea. In 1950, a nearby volcano erupted and destroyed much of the butterfly's forest habitat, so it is now endangered (EN).

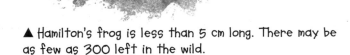

Male

▶ Like many tropical butterflies, the female and male Queen Alexandra's birdwing look quite different from each other.

Female

I DON'T BELIEVE IT!
The Bermuda petrel was thought to be extinct for over 300 years until a breeding group was discovered on some coastal rocks in 1951.

The greatest threat

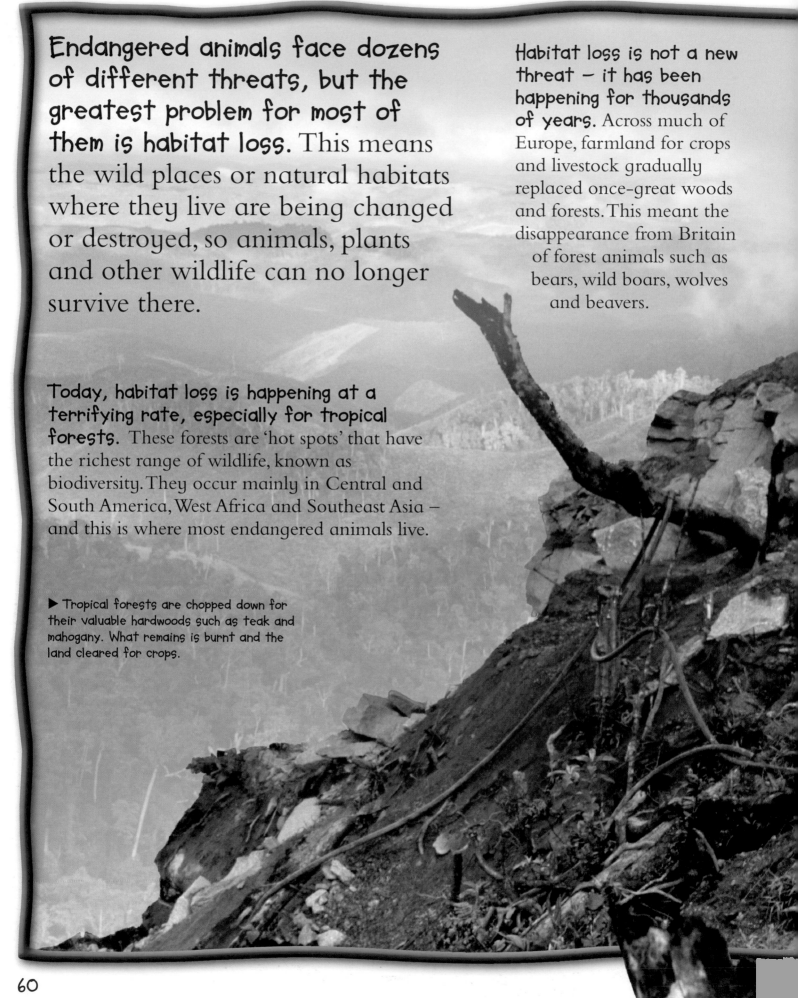

Endangered animals face dozens of different threats, but the greatest problem for most of them is habitat loss. This means the wild places or natural habitats where they live are being changed or destroyed, so animals, plants and other wildlife can no longer survive there.

Today, habitat loss is happening at a terrifying rate, especially for tropical forests. These forests are 'hot spots' that have the richest range of wildlife, known as biodiversity. They occur mainly in Central and South America, West Africa and Southeast Asia – and this is where most endangered animals live.

▶ Tropical forests are chopped down for their valuable hardwoods such as teak and mahogany. What remains is burnt and the land cleared for crops.

Habitat loss is not a new threat – it has been happening for thousands of years. Across much of Europe, farmland for crops and livestock gradually replaced once-great woods and forests. This meant the disappearance from Britain of forest animals such as bears, wild boars, wolves and beavers.

The muriquis or woolly spider monkeys of Brazil are critically endangered. Trees in their tropical forests have been chopped down for logs and the timber trade. Then the land is cleared for farm animals and crops. The monkeys, along with thousands of other forest species, have fewer places to live.

In Borneo, animals from pygmy elephants to orang-utans are under threat as their forests are cleared for oil palm trees and other crops. Oil palm plantations are one of the main reasons for habitat loss across the tropics. The vegetable oil from the fleshy fruits is used for cooking, to make margarine and prepared meals, and for a vehicle fuel known as biodiesel.

61

Too many people

Many animals no longer live in their natural habitats because people now live there. The number of people in the world increases by about 150 every minute. They need houses, land for farms, shops, schools, factories and roads. More people means less places for wildlife.

Animals living in lakes, rivers, marshes and swamps are some of the most endangered. Their habitats are drained and cleared for towns, ports and waterside holiday centres. Tourist areas along rivers and coastlines endanger all kinds of animals.

▼ Across the world, cities spread into nearby natural habitats, such as this shanty town in Colombia, South America.

QUIZ

Can you name the major threats these animals face?
1. Mediterranean monk seal
2. Red panda
3. Black-necked crane
4. Golden bamboo lemur

Answers:
1. Spread of holiday areas along the Mediterranean 2. Loss of bamboo 3. Tourists 4. Loss of trees in Madagascar due to spreading villages and farms

The Mediterranean monk seal has suffered greatly from the spread of tourism. Its breeding and resting areas have been taken over for holiday villages, sunbathing beaches and water sports. This seal has also been hunted by fishermen, who believe it 'steals' their fish, and affected by pollution. It is now critical, with fewer than 600 left.

▲ The shy Mediterranean monk seal is frightened by boats and divers, and tries to hide in underwater caves.

◄ Black-necked cranes are sometimes poisoned by pesticide chemicals used by farmers.

The black-necked crane lives in the highlands around the Himalayas in Asia. It faces several threats. One is the development of tourism in a region known as the Ladakh Valley in India. People come to gaze at the marvellous scenery and watch the wildlife, but they disturb the cranes, who are shy and less likely to breed.

The giant panda is a famous rare animal, and its distant cousin, the red panda, is also under threat. This tree-dwelling bamboo-eater from South and East Asia has fewer places to live, as towns and villages spread quickly. It's also hunted for its fur, especially its bushy tail, which is used to make hats and good luck wedding charms.

► The red panda is fully protected by law, but hunting continues for its fur.

Pollution problems

Pollution is a threat to all wildlife, as the wastes and chemicals we make get into the air, soil and water. Like many dangers to animals, pollution is often combined with other threats, such as habitat loss and climate change. Sometimes it is difficult to separate these dangers, since one is part of another.

▲ This Atlantic croaker fish has become blind with misty eyes, or cataracts, due to chemicals in the water.

Harmful chemicals spread quickly through water to affect streams, rivers, lakes and even the open ocean. Caspian seals live in the landlocked Caspian Sea, a vast lake in West Asia. Industries and factories around the lake shore pollute its waters. The seals suffer from sores and fur loss, and are less resistant to diseases.

◀ Oil spillages are a devastating form of pollution. This beaver is covered in oil, which it tries to lick from its coat. By doing so it swallows poisonous chemicals that may kill it.

The largest amphibians in the world are Chinese and Japanese giant salamanders. They are in danger from pollution of their cool, fast-flowing, highland streams. There are few factories there, but the clouds and rains carry polluting chemicals from the smoke and fumes of factory chimneys far away.

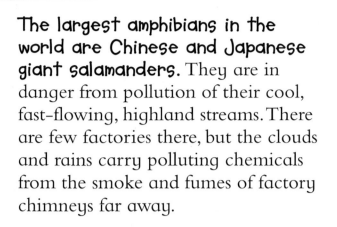

▼ The baiji's home in the Yangtze River has become a dangerous, polluted place. The last sighting of one of these dolphins was in 2004.

POLLUTION HAZARDS

Next time you are in the park or countryside, look out for types of pollution. Find out how they could harm animals, and how we can reduce them. Look for examples such as:

Litter in ponds • Plastic bags in bushes and hedges • Pools of oil or fuel from vehicles Broken glass • Pipes carrying poisonous liquids into ditches, streams or rivers • Metal wire, plastic tags and similar objects

A survey in 2006 failed to find any baijis, or Chinese river dolphins. One of the threats to this dolphin is pollution of its main river, the Yangtze or Chang Jiang, by factories along its banks, and by farm chemicals seeping into the water from fields. The pollution has harmed not only the baiji but also the fish and other animals that it eats. Further threats include hunting by people for its meat, the building of dams, drowning in fishing nets and being hit by boats.

Baiji (Chinese river dolphin)

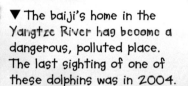

A change in the weather

The whole world faces climate change, which could endanger many animal species. The weather is gradually becoming warmer because our atmosphere (the layer of air around Earth) is being altered by 'greenhouse gases'. These come mainly from burning fuels such as petrol, diesel, wood, coal and natural gas. They make the Earth trap heat from the Sun, and so the planet gets hotter.

In the far north, polar bears are threatened because ice floes (big lumps of ice) are melting faster. The bears use the ice floes to hunt seals from and to rest on. There used to be plenty of floes, but now polar bears can swim for hours before finding one. Some bears even drown, exhausted in the open sea.

In the far south, penguins have trouble finding icebergs to rest on. As in the north, the icebergs melt faster due to global warming. Like the polar bears, the penguins cannot get out of the water for a rest, and because they cannot fly, they may drown.

▶ Fewer, smaller ice floes spell terrible trouble for polar bears.

▼ Penguins become tired after feeding in the water for several hours, and need to rest on the shore or an iceberg. Global warming means that the ice is melting and penguins' resting places are disappearing.

Global warming is changing the seasons, which may affect huge numbers of animals. An earlier spring means that insects in Europe breed a week or two before they used to. However, migrating birds from Africa, such as pied flycatchers, swallows and swifts, might arrive too late to catch the insects for their chicks. Scientists call this 'uncoupling' of the natural links between animals and their seasonal food.

The huge Asian fish, the beluga sturgeon, is already endangered. It is poached for the female's eggs, which are sold as the expensive food caviar. However, as global warming continues, the sturgeon's rivers and lakes will be affected, which could push the fish to extinction even more quickly.

I DON'T BELIEVE IT!

Scientists studying 40,000 tree swallows say that the birds now lay their eggs nine days earlier than they did 40 years ago, probably as a result of global warming.

▲ Beluga sturgeons used to grow to more than 5 metres long, but most of them are now caught and killed before they reach such a great size.

Poaching and souvenirs

◀ Weight for weight, rhino horn can be worth more than gems such as rubies and pearls.

The main reason that rhinos are so endangered is because of poaching for their horns. The horns are carved into decorative objects such as dagger handles, or ground down to make traditional Chinese medicine. The most common use is to bring down fevers – although there is little scientific proof this works.

Some animals are endangered because they are hunted for trophies, souvenirs, and body parts. Poaching is the illegal killing of animals for their body parts, such as elephants for their ivory tusks.

MATCH UP

Can you match the animals with the products they are killed or captured for?

A. Tiger
B. Elephant
C. Giant clam
D. Rhino

1. Dagger handle
2. Tourist souvenir
3. Bones
4. Ivory

Answers:
A3 B4 C2 D1

68

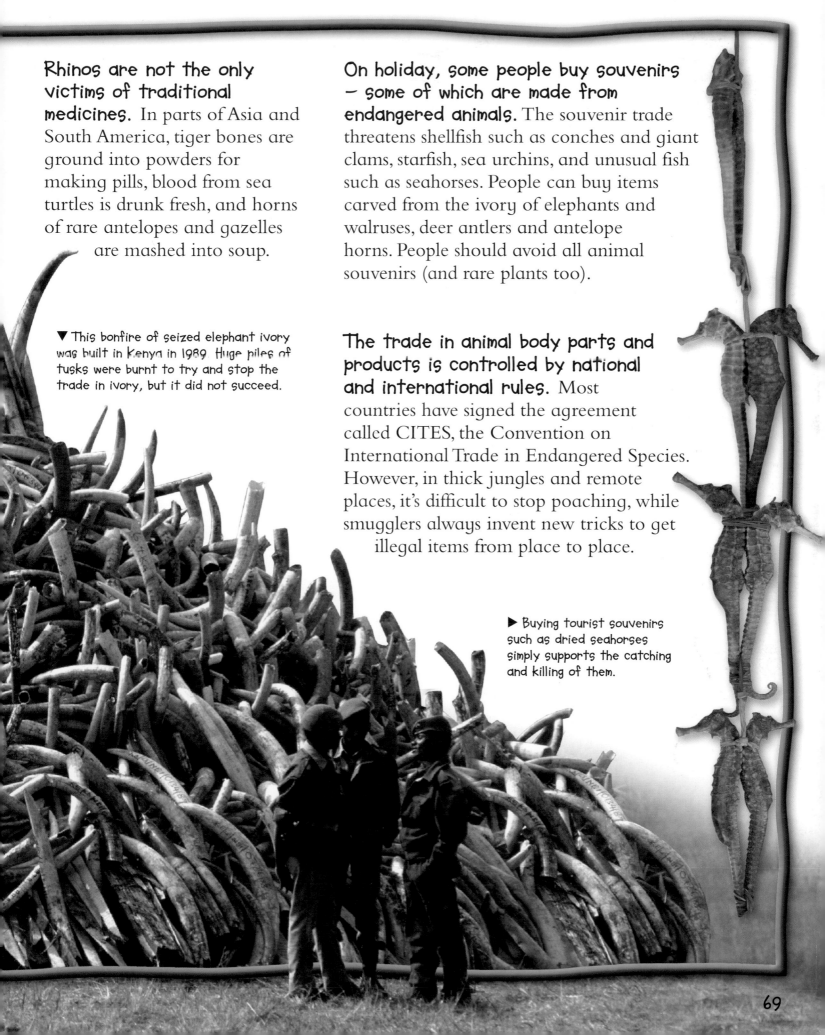

Rhinos are not the only victims of traditional medicines. In parts of Asia and South America, tiger bones are ground into powders for making pills, blood from sea turtles is drunk fresh, and horns of rare antelopes and gazelles are mashed into soup.

▼ This bonfire of seized elephant ivory was built in Kenya in 1989. Huge piles of tusks were burnt to try and stop the trade in ivory, but it did not succeed.

On holiday, some people buy souvenirs – some of which are made from endangered animals. The souvenir trade threatens shellfish such as conches and giant clams, starfish, sea urchins, and unusual fish such as seahorses. People can buy items carved from the ivory of elephants and walruses, deer antlers and antelope horns. People should avoid all animal souvenirs (and rare plants too).

The trade in animal body parts and products is controlled by national and international rules. Most countries have signed the agreement called CITES, the Convention on International Trade in Endangered Species. However, in thick jungles and remote places, it's difficult to stop poaching, while smugglers always invent new tricks to get illegal items from place to place.

► Buying tourist souvenirs such as dried seahorses simply supports the catching and killing of them.

Kill or be killed

Some animals are endangered because of the threat they pose to people – at least, that is the belief. Big, powerful predators are seen as dangerous to people, pets and farm animals. The risk of possible attack leads to persecution and revenge killing of the animal species. Hunters become the hunted.

In Central and South America, the jaguar, a spotted big cat, is often killed because of the risk that it might attack farm animals. Large areas of forest are cleared for cattle grazing, and some ranchers hire professional jaguar hunters who shoot the big cats on sight. Jaguars used to be killed for another reason – their beautiful fur coats. However, trade in jaguar fur and other body parts is now illegal.

◄ In parts of South America, hunters kill small crocodiles called caimans to sell their skins and flesh, even though it's against the law.

Crocodiles and alligators are shot because of the threats they pose to people and their animals. The endangered Cuban crocodile lives in only a small region of rivers and swamps on the Caribbean island of Cuba. It is a small crocodile, about 2 to 2.5 metres long. However, it has long been hunted because of the danger of attack, as well as for its meat and skin.

▶ Great white sharks can be lured to their death by baits.

The great white shark is one of the most feared of all animals. People hunt and kill it just in case it attacks swimmers. This shark is now rare enough to be on the Red List of threatened species as VU, vulnerable.

I DON'T BELIEVE IT!

About 100 years ago there were probably more than 100,000 tigers. Now there are probably fewer than 5000 in the wild.

▼ Like any hungry predator, a tiger will take advantage of a weak farm animal such as a sheep.

Tigers face many threats, especially habitat loss, poaching and being killed in case they become 'man-eaters'. As villages and farms spread, tigers have less natural prey, and they are also more likely to wander near people and farm livestock. Another major threat is being poached for their body parts, such as their bones, teeth and bile (liver fluid) to put in traditional medicines. This fate probably affects one tiger every day.

71

Eaten to extinction?

The bushmeat trade – hunting wild animals for food – is a growing threat to many species. People have always ventured into the forest to kill wild animals to eat. However modern rifles, traps and other weapons mean that more animals can be caught, and sold at market. This growing trade in commercial bushmeat has become a huge problem.

In Africa, the drill and mandrill are the world's largest monkeys, and both are in huge danger from the bushmeat trade. Killing one of these animals and selling most of its meat provides enough money to buy a week's food for a family.

▲ Bushmeat is sold at many local markets such as this one in West Africa. Once the animals have been skinned and cut up, it's difficult to identify if they are protected.

▼ For thousands of years, local people have caught and eaten animals, such as this monkey, from the forests around them.

I DON'T BELIEVE IT!

The blackbuck antelope is protected in India. It was introduced to the US, and it breeds so well on ranches that numbers have to be reduced. So it's eaten in restaurants, and spare blackbucks are sent back to India to keep up the numbers.

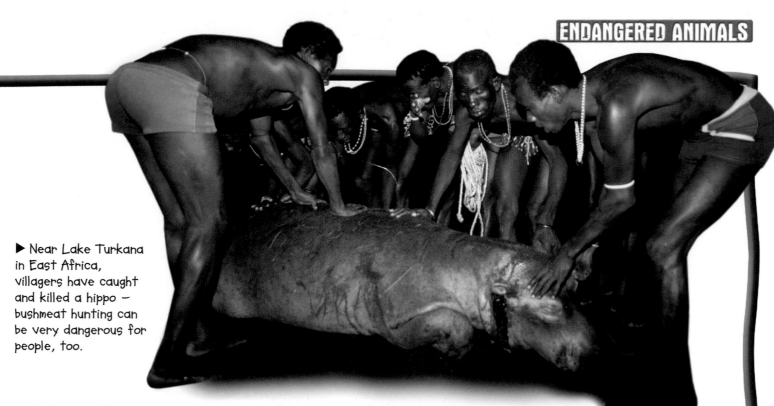

▶ Near Lake Turkana in East Africa, villagers have caught and killed a hippo — bushmeat hunting can be very dangerous for people, too.

In West Africa, the pygmy hippo is endangered due to hunting for its meat. This small hippo lives in thick forests and travels along regular tracks to and from its feeding areas. If hunters find a track, they lie in wait for their prey. Fewer than 3000 pygmy hippos are left in the wild.

In South America, the Brazilian tapir's flesh is considered a delicacy, so it is a prize target for bushmeat hunters. It is VU, vulnerable, but its cousin, the mountain tapir, is even more at risk. There are less than 2500 in the wild and better protection is needed.

▶ In West Africa, logging vehicles leaving the forest are checked for animals captured for the bushmeat trade.

Mainly in India, and through most of Southeast Asia, bushmeat hunting is affecting more animals. The thamin, or Eld's deer, is listed as VU, vulnerable. In some places they have so little forest left that they eat farm crops. Local people kill them to stop the crop damage — and to have a meal.

Threats for pets

Some animals are endangered because they are caught from the wild to become pets or captives. There is a thriving illegal trade in supplying rare animals as pets, and to personal collectors and private zoos. It is not only illegal but also cruel and wasteful. Many of the animals suffer and die on the long journeys to their new homes.

▼ Criminals dig up and steal the eggs of the Komodo dragon, which fetch large sums of money in the illegal collecting trade.

▲ Exotic pets, such as this macaw, often travel in terrible conditions, cramped and dirty, with little or no food and water. They end up in cages where they often die.

The world's biggest lizard, the endangered Komodo dragon, has its eggs stolen from the wild by thieves. These are sold to egg collectors, reptile breeders and lizard fanciers. This is illegal, but some people cannot resist the thrill of having such a rare egg, even if they must keep it secret.

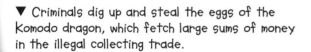

Colourful, clever birds such as parrots and macaws are sometimes caught for the caged bird trade, rather than being bred in captivity. Rare species such as the hyacinth macaw, the biggest of all the parrots, and the green-winged macaw, are taken from the wild. It is against the law, but bird collectors pay huge amounts for them.

QUIZ

1. What is the world's biggest lizard?
2. Why is this lizard endangered?
3. What is the world's biggest parrot?
4. What is the world's biggest frog?

Answers:
1. Komodo dragon 2. Because people steal its eggs to sell 3. Hyacinth macaw 4. Goliath frog

◄ This tilapia cichlid fish has a been caught from the wild and placed in an aquarium. It has a burn mark on its back from resting too near to the aquarium lights.

Various tropical fish are caught from rivers and lakes for the aquarium trade. Some of the rarest are the tilapia cichlid fishes of the African Rift Valley lakes. Responsible aquarium suppliers and respected pet stores know about threatened species and do not accept those caught in the wild.

The world's biggest frog, the Goliath frog of Africa, is taken from the wild and sold to amphibian fanciers and private collectors. Its head and body are 30 centimetres long, and it can leap 6 metres in one jump. Being so large, this frog is also a good catch for the bushmeat trade.

► In West Africa, Goliath frogs — classed as endangered, EN — are caught in nets or traps. Their numbers are thought to have halved in the past 20 years.

Island problems

Many threatened animals live on islands. Here, the creatures and plants have lived together for many years. They have changed, or evolved, to become specialized to their unique habitat. The small size of many islands means less animals, and the unique habitat is easily upset when people arrive.

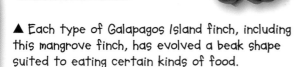

Mangrove finch

▲ Each type of Galapagos Island finch, including this mangrove finch, has evolved a beak shape suited to eating certain kinds of food.

The mangrove finch, which lives on the Galapagos Islands in the Pacific Ocean, is critically endangered. It is one of Darwin's finches – the birds that helped English naturalist Charles Darwin (1809–1882) work out his theory of evolution, which is so important to science.

Also on the Galapagos, giant tortoises are under threat, partly due to a common island problem – introduced species. People have taken many animals to islands, such as cats, rats, rabbits and dogs. These new arrivals destroy the natural habitat, prey on some local species, and compete for food and shelter.

▶ 'Lonesome George' is the last of his kind – a Pinta Island giant Galapagos tortoise. When he dies, the species will no longer exist.

The island of Madagascar has amazing and unique wildlife, but much of it is in danger. Lemurs, such as the ring-tailed lemur, are found nowhere else in the wild. However, many Madagascan species are threatened by a mixture of habitat loss, hunting for food, capture for the illegal pet trade, and the problem of introduced species.

◄ Ring-tailed lemurs are popular in wildlife parks and zoos, but are becoming rarer on their island home of Madagascar.

On islands, not just exciting species such as giant tortoises and colourful birds are threatened. There are less glamorous species, such as the partula snails of the South Pacific islands. They were eaten by a predatory snail called Euglandina, which was introduced to provide food for local people.

There have been more than 700 known animal extinctions in the last 400 years — and about half of these were on islands. In the Hawaiian islands alone about 25 kinds of birds, 70 types of snails, 80 kinds of insects and more than 100 plants have disappeared in the past 200 years.

► Some species of partula snails now survive only in zoos or science laboratories.

Stop the slaughter

For more than 50 years there has been a growing awareness of endangered animals and how we can save them. 'Headline' species such as pandas, whales, tigers and gorillas grab the interest of people and help to raise money for conservation. This conservation work can then protect natural habitats and so save many other species as well.

▲ The Born Free Foundation is an international wildlife charity working around the world to protect threatened species in the wild.

In the 1960s, the giant panda of China became famous as the symbol of the World Wildlife Fund, WWF (now World Wide Fund for Nature). Huge conservation efforts mean the giant panda is now off the critical list, with some 2000 in the wild, although it is still listed as EN, endangered.

◀ Pandas eat almost nothing but particular kinds of bamboo, so they rely heavily on their specialized habitat.

I DON'T BELIEVE IT!

The giant panda was chosen as a symbol of conservation partly because of its black-and-white colours. These make its image easier to photocopy without the need for any colours.

In the 1970s, people started to protest against the commercial hunting of great whales, which was threatening many whale species. 'Save the Whale' campaigns and marches became popular. Eventually in 1980 there was a world ban on the mass hunting of large whales.

In the 1990s, the terrible crisis facing the tiger became clear. Save the Tiger Fund was founded in 1995 to fight the many dangers facing the biggest of big cats. However, it is too late for some varieties, or subspecies, of tiger. The Balinese tiger from the island of Bali became extinct in the 1930s, and the Javan tiger followed in the 1980s.

▶ Great whales, such as these blue whales, are now fairly safe from mass slaughter. However, they breed very slowly and their numbers will take many years to start rising again.

In the 1980s, there were many anti-fur campaigns, to stop the killing of wild cats and other animals for their fur coats. This helped to reduce one of the threats to many beautiful cat species, not only big cats, but also medium and small species such as the ocelot and margay. Sadly, fur is becoming a popular fashion item once more.

A place to live

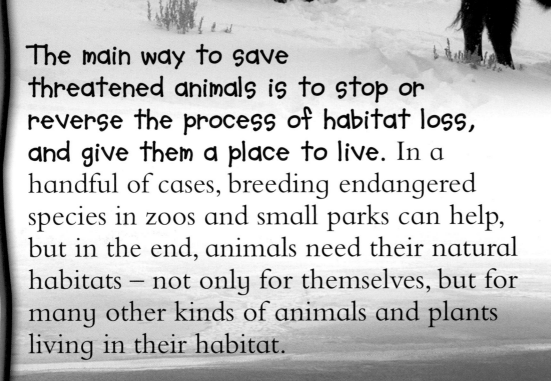

The main way to save threatened animals is to stop or reverse the process of habitat loss, and give them a place to live. In a handful of cases, breeding endangered species in zoos and small parks can help, but in the end, animals need their natural habitats – not only for themselves, but for many other kinds of animals and plants living in their habitat.

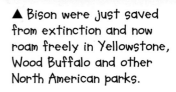

▲ Bison were just saved from extinction and now roam freely in Yellowstone, Wood Buffalo and other North American parks.

▼ The Great Barrier Reef Marine Park has gradually been extended over the years, with limited tourism in some areas and complete protection in others.

Natural places are preserved by setting aside large areas as national parks, nature reserves and wildlife sanctuaries. In 1872, Yellowstone National Park in the USA became the world's first national park. As in other protected areas, there are laws preventing people from damaging the animals, plants or habitat. Yellowstone's animals include the American bison or 'buffalo', which used to roam the prairies in millions. It almost became extinct in the 1880s but was just saved.

Some of the most important and precious wild areas are given the title of World Heritage Site. In Ethiopia, East Africa, the Simien National Park is home to extremely rare animals such as the gelada baboon, the Ethiopian wolf (Simien fox or jackal), and a type of wild goat called the Walia ibex, of which there are only 500 left.

▲ The 500 surviving Ethiopian wolves are found in only a few areas, such as the Bale Mountains and Simien National Park in Ethiopia.

One of the world's biggest protected ocean areas is Australia's Great Barrier Reef Marine Park, home to amazing animals from tiny coral creatures to huge sharks. In 2006 the US set up the even bigger NorthWest Hawaiian Island National Monument. This reserve is home to more than 7000 animal species including the threatened Hawaiian monk seal, green turtle and Laysan albatross.

QUIZ

Where would you find these rare animals?

1. Ethiopian wolf
2. American bison
3. Hawaiian monk seal
4. Green turtle

Answers:
1. Simien National Park, Ethiopia 2. Yellowstone National Park, USA 3. NorthWest Hawaiian Island National Monument 4. Great Barrier Reef, Australia

Captive breeding

Zoos, wildlife parks and breeding centres may play an important role in saving animals. Some animals are kept and encouraged to breed and build up their numbers, hopefully for release back into the wild. This method needs expert knowledge about the species, so the zoo keepers can look after the animals well. However, it can only be used in selected cases.

Not only big exciting animals are bred in captivity — one of the smallest is the Chatham Island black robin. By the early 1980s, only five remained, with just one female, 'Old Blue'. Careful captive breeding involved taking away her first batch of eggs, so she would lay a second clutch, while keepers cared for the first batch so they hatched. There are now more than 250 black robins.

▼ When rare animals such as the giant panda are reared in captivity, scientists can learn much about them.

◀ Pere David's deer have been released back into their home area of China.

For many years, Pere David's deer lived only in reserves owned by the emperors of China. Gradually the deer disappeared – many were eaten. However, a few were taken to Woburn animal park in the UK, where they bred. In the 1980s, some Pere David's deer were released back into the wild in China, where they are still CR, critically endangered.

The critically endangered Grand Cayman Blue Iguana was down to fewer than 15 lizards. Since 1996, captive-bred lizards have been released into protected areas on the island of Grand Cayman, and more reserves and releases are planned.

▼ Blue Iguanas are tagged so they can be closely monitored in their protected areas.

▼ Tigers breed well in some zoos, but release into the wild is virtually impossible. Captive tigers lose their instinct to kill, so may starve to death.

There are many problems when releasing captive-bred animals back into the wild, especially for apes such as orang-utans. Young apes learn from their parents about how to find food and avoid danger. If they are brought up in captivity they may need to be taught by people how to become wild again.

Future help

▼ Whale-watching not only helps people to appreciate the wonders of these great animals, but also how important it is to save all natural places and their wildlife.

Saving threatened animals is not just for wildlife organizations and governments — everyone can help. You could volunteer for a conservation group, or set up a wildlife club in your school or neighbourhood. You might raise awareness by telling family and friends about threatened species, or have a 'rare animals' birthday party.

Local zoos and wildlife parks often have lots of information about endangered animals and their conservation. You can visit, write or email them, to ask if they are involved in conservation. Find out how zoos share information about their rare animals, so suitable individuals can be brought together for breeding. Wildlife conservation organizations often offer animal adoptions so you can sponsor a rare animal, maybe as a birthday present or a gift.

Saving threatened animals cannot be done without saving their habitats — and taking into account people. The people who live in the same area as a rare species may be very poor and very hungry. They see lots of time and money being spent on the endangered animal, but nothing for themselves.

Countries and governments must take into account their people, animals, plants and habitats, for a long-term and sustainable result. For example, wildlife can help to raise money by encouraging environmentally responsible tourism. This is when people pay to see rare creatures, such as gorillas, whales and tigers, under careful, monitored conditions. Then the money is used for local conservation that helps people as well as wildlife. Only in this way can people and endangered animals live together for the future.

I DON'T BELIEVE IT!

In 2005, a new kind of monkey, the highland mangabey, was discovered in Africa. At the same time it became one of the rarest and most threatened of all animal species.

▶ A close-up view of a tiger can encourage tourists to support campaigns to save these beautiful animals, and thereby protect large areas of their habitat for other creatures and plants.

EXTINCT

Extinction is when all individuals of one kind of living thing die out forever, so there are no more alive. It usually applies to a whole species (kind) of living thing, not just to one individual. Extinction has happened for billions of years since life on Earth began. Scientists estimate that 999 out of every 1000 kinds of living things that have ever existed have become extinct. Today, the number of extinctions is speeding up because of what people are doing to the natural world.

▼ Giant dragonflies, millipedes as big as dining tables and enormous tree ferns once inhabited forests 300 million years ago. However all of the creatures in this prehistoric swamp have long been extinct.

What is extinction?

Extinction is the dying out of a particular kind, or type, of living thing. It is gone forever and can never come back (although this may change in the future). Extinction affects plants such as flowers and trees, as well as fungi such as mushrooms and moulds. It also affects tiny worms and bugs, and big creatures such as dinosaurs and mammoths.

▲ The 'terror bird' *Phorusrhacos* lived ten million years ago. Nothing like it survives today.

▲ There were hundreds of kinds of sea scorpions (eurypterids) 250 million years ago, but all died out.

Extinction is linked to how we classify (group) living things. It usually applies to a species. A species includes all living things that look similar and breed to produce more of their kind. For instance, all lions belong to one species, which scientists call *Panthera leo*.

QUIZ

Which of these could, perhaps, one day become extinct?
1. Great white sharks 2. Robots
3. Daisies 4. Cameras with rolls of film (not digital)
5. Satellites 6. Houseflies

Answers:
Only living things can become extinct, so the answers are 1, 3 and 6

One example of an extinct species is the giant elk *Megaloceros giganteus* of the last Ice Age. The last ones died out almost 8000 years ago. But not all elk species became extinct. A similar but separate species, the elk (moose) *Alces alces*, is still alive today.

Sometimes extinction affects a subspecies. This is a group of animals within a species that are all very similar, and slightly different from others in the species. All tigers today belong to one species, *Panthera tigris*. There were once eight subspecies of tiger. Two have become extinct in the past 100 years, the Balinese tiger and the Javan tiger.

► All six living subspecies of tiger differ slightly – and all are threatened with extinction.

Bengal tiger

South China tiger

▲ The last Balinese tiger, the smallest subspecies, was killed in 1937.

Siberian tiger

Extinction can also affect a group of closely related species, which is called a genus. There have been about ten species of mammoths over the last two million years. They all belonged to the genus *Mammuthus*, including the woolly mammoth and the steppe mammoth. All mammoths have died out, so the genus is extinct.

◄ The Columbian mammoth, one of the biggest in the genus, died out by 12,000 years ago.

Sumatran tiger

Malayan tiger

Indochinese tiger

Extinction and evolution

Extinctions have happened through billions of years of prehistory as a natural part of evolution. Evolution is the gradual change in living things, resulting in new species appearing. As this happened, other species could not survive and became extinct.

◀ Today's hagfish differ little from their extinct cousins millions of years ago, but they are a separate species.

Evolution occurs as the result of changing conditions. Living things adapt to become better suited to conditions as they change, such as the weather and types of habitats (living places).

▶ Unlike the hagfish, the extinct armoured fish *Hemicyclaspis* from 400 million years ago has no living relatives.

I DON'T BELIEVE IT!

Trilobites were a group of marine creatures that survived for almost 300 million years. Within that time at least 18,000 kinds came and went. The last trilobites died out in a mass extinction 250 million years ago.

90

Angelina
490 million years ago

Trinucleus
450 million years ago

Kolihapeltis
400 million years ago

▲ Many different kinds of trilobites evolved and died out over millions of years.

Scientists know about long-gone extinct species from their fossils. These are remains of body parts such as the bones, teeth, horns, claws and shells of animals, and the bark, roots and leaves of plants, which have been preserved in rocks and turned to stone.

Studying millions of fossils of thousands of extinct species all around the world shows how different kinds of living things came and went long ago. This 'turnover' of species gives the average rate of extinction. For every one million species, one species would die out about once each year.

▲ Scientists have studied more than one million trilobite fossils.

▶ *Stegosaurus* was one of the longest-lasting dinosaur species. Its kind survived for over ten million years.

▼ Magnolias are flowering plants that have successfully evolved from 100 million years ago to today.

Fossil studies show the typical time for a species or genus to survive before going extinct. A mammal species lasted from one to two million years. For sea-living invertebrates (creatures without backbones) such as crabs, species survived between five and ten million years.

Why does it happen?

There are several reasons for extinction. Many extinctions are combinations of these reasons. We cannot know for sure why prehistoric species became extinct. But we can see the reasons for extinctions today. These may help us to understand what happened in the past.

One reason for extinction is competition. A species cannot get enough of its needs, such as food or living space, because other species need them too, and are better at getting them. These competing species may be newly evolved, or may have spread from afar.

A species can be forced to extinction by predators, parasites or diseases. Again, all of these could be new dangers as a result of evolution.

▼ In Australia, introduced farm animals such as sheep, and also wild rabbits, have been better than local species at gaining food.

▲ Australia's rock wallabies have suffered due to competition from sheep and goats.

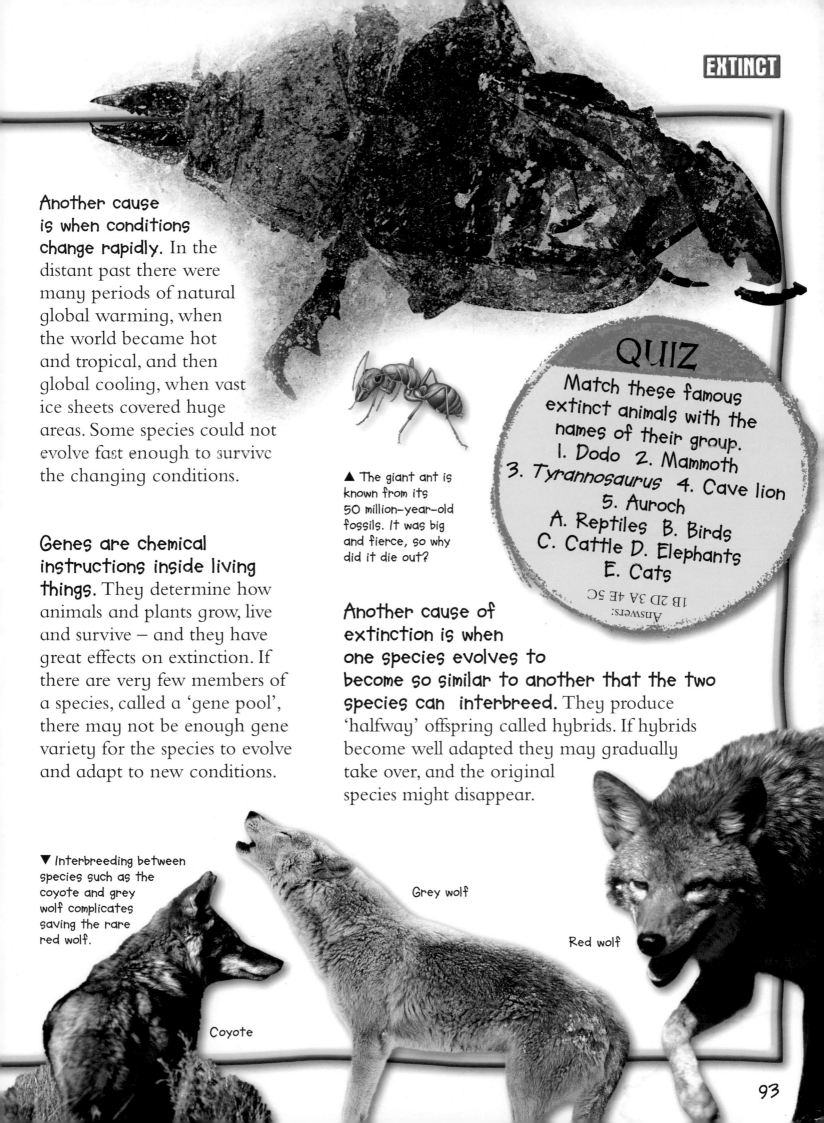

Another cause is when conditions change rapidly. In the distant past there were many periods of natural global warming, when the world became hot and tropical, and then global cooling, when vast ice sheets covered huge areas. Some species could not evolve fast enough to survive the changing conditions.

Genes are chemical instructions inside living things. They determine how animals and plants grow, live and survive – and they have great effects on extinction. If there are very few members of a species, called a 'gene pool', there may not be enough gene variety for the species to evolve and adapt to new conditions.

▲ The giant ant is known from its 50 million-year-old fossils. It was big and fierce, so why did it die out?

QUIZ
Match these famous extinct animals with the names of their group.
1. Dodo 2. Mammoth
3. Tyrannosaurus 4. Cave lion
5. Auroch
A. Reptiles B. Birds
C. Cattle D. Elephants
E. Cats

Answers:
1B 2D 3A 4E 5C

Another cause of extinction is when one species evolves to become so similar to another that the two species can interbreed. They produce 'halfway' offspring called hybrids. If hybrids become well adapted they may gradually take over, and the original species might disappear.

▼ Interbreeding between species such as the coyote and grey wolf complicates saving the rare red wolf.

Grey wolf

Red wolf

Coyote

How do we Know?

How do we know if a species is extinct?

The more recent the extinction, the harder it is to say. How long should we wait before saying a species is extinct? It might be found living in a remote area years later.

Wildlife experts at the IUCN (International Union for Conservation of Nature) say that a species cannot be declared extinct until 50 years have passed with no real sightings of it, or evidence such as droppings or eggshells.

▲ Leadbeater's possums were restricted to a very small area, as land around was turned into farms.

Sometimes, a species thought to be extinct 'comes back from the dead'. Usually it has survived in an unexplored area. It is called a 'Lazarus species' after a man in the Bible who came to life again after he died.

One 'Lazarus species' is the squirrel-like Leadbeater's possum of Australia. It was thought to be extinct by the 1930s, but in 1965, a group was found living in highland forests in southeast Australia. Plant 'Lazarus species' include the jellyfish tree and Monte Diablo buckwheat.

Some people consider creatures such as the yeti (abominable snowman), bunyip and Bigfoot to be extinct. But most scientists would say that these creatures are only from tales and legends. There is no real scientific proof they ever lived, so they cannot be extinct.

Some species are 'extinct in the wild'. This means all surviving members are in zoos, wildlife parks or gardens. One example is the toromiro, a tree that disappeared from Easter Island in the Pacific. Experts saved some at Kew Gardens, London, and it is now being taken back to its original home.

▶ A toromiro flower. The toromiro tree once covered parts of Easter Island, but it was wiped out in the wild.

▲ The huge, hairy yeti of the Himalayas is well known in myths and stories, but no real evidence of its existance has been discovered.

▼ In 1987, only 22 Californian condors were left in the wild. All were captured for breeding and chicks were raised using 'condor parent' puppet gloves.

FAME AT LAST

You will need:
books about Australia
the Internet

Look in books or on the Internet for information about the state of Victoria in Australia. See if you can find the state's animal emblem or symbol, and a picture of it. That's Leadbeater's possum!

Not quite extinct

◀ Pterosaurs (pterodactyls) were flying reptiles that died out with the dinosaurs 65 million years ago.

It's easy to decide if prehistoric species are extinct. No one has seen living dinosaurs. Some myths and legends say they exist, but there's no scientific proof. So we assume all dinosaurs are extinct.

Living species (such as the coelacanth) that are very similar to long-extinct ones are known as 'living fossils'. They help us to understand how evolution works and how the original species may have become extinct.

Some 'Lazarus species' lived millions of years ago in prehistoric times, but have been recently rediscovered. Fossils show that the coelacanth fish died out over 60 million years ago. In 1938 one was caught off southeast Africa, with more seen since.

▼ Coelacanth fish of today are not exactly the same species from millions of years ago, but very similar.

I DON'T BELIEVE IT!

The coelacanth is not one living fossil species — it is two! The African coelacanth is found in the west Indian Ocean. Across this ocean is the Indonesian coelacanth.

► The Chacoan peccary is similar to the giant Ice Age peccary that disappeared 10,000 years ago.

When a particular species is known to be living, it is called 'extant' rather than 'extinct'. Other examples of extant 'living fossils' include Australia's Wollemi pine tree, the pig-like Chacoan peccary, and the shellfish known as the lampshell.

A tree 'living fossil' once thought to be extinct is the dawn redwood. It was known only from fossils dating back ten million years. Then in 1944, examples were found in China. The living species, *Metasequoia glyptostroboides,* is slightly different to the long-extinct species.

◄ Large copper butterflies are still found in mainland Europe, but habitats lost to farming mean they are rare.

► The dawn redwood, one of only three redwood species, is now planted in parks and gardens across the world.

A particular plant or creature may become extinct in one area but be extant in another. In Europe the large copper butterfly became extinct in Britain in the 1860s, but it still lives in many other places across the region.

Beliefs and ideas

The way people view extinction has changed through the ages. Scientists' thoughts can be very different to those of other people. Some people don't believe in extinction, perhaps due to religious ideas.

As people began to study fossils, they realized that they were from living things that were no longer around. Some experts said these plants and animals survived somewhere remote and undiscovered. Others began to suggest that extinction really did happen.

In ancient times, people such as the Greek scientist-naturalist Aristotle (384–322 BC) believed that the natural world had never changed. No new species evolved and no old ones became extinct.

Fossil expert Georges Cuvier (1769–1832) was one of the first scientists to say that there probably were extinctions. Due to his religious beliefs, he explained them as happening in the Great Floods described in the Bible.

▼ Baron Georges Cuvier admitted that the fossil elephants he studied had become extinct.

GOOD AND BAD EXTINCTIONS

Make a list of animals that can cause problems such as spreading diseases, eating farmers' crops and damaging trees. Ask your family and friends: If you could make some extinct, which ones would you choose and why? Does everyone have the same answers? Here's a few to get you started: Houseflies, fleas, rats, squirrels, pigeons, foxes, deer.

▲ By altering the malaria-carrying mosquito's genes, scientists may be able to wipe out the disease malaria.

▼ In South America, Darwin studied fossils of the giant armadillo-like *Glyptodon* and wondered why it no longer survived.

Modern views continue to change about extinction. Scientists can now identify separate species by studying their genes, rather than what they look like or how they breed. What was thought to be one species could, with genetic information, be two or more. For endangered plants and animals, it might not be one species threatened with extinction, but several.

In 1859, extinction became an important topic. Naturalist Charles Darwin described the theory of evolution in his book *On the Origin of Species by Means of Natural Selection*. In it Darwin explained the idea of 'survival of the fittest', and how new species evolved while other species less equipped to deal with their environment died out.

▶ A scene from the 2009 movie *Creation*. Darwin's ideas about evolution shaped modern scientific views on extinction.

Long, long ago

The history of life on Earth dates back over three billion years, and extinction has been happening since then. Millions of plants and animals have died out over this time, called the geological timescale.

Fossil evidence shows that even 500 million years ago, there was an enormous variety of life with many species becoming extinct. The idea that long ago there were just a few species, which gradually increased through to today, with new ones evolving but very few dying out, is not accurate.

▼ Spiny sharks such as *Acanthodes* flourished in Devonian times but gradually died out.

Acanthodes fossil

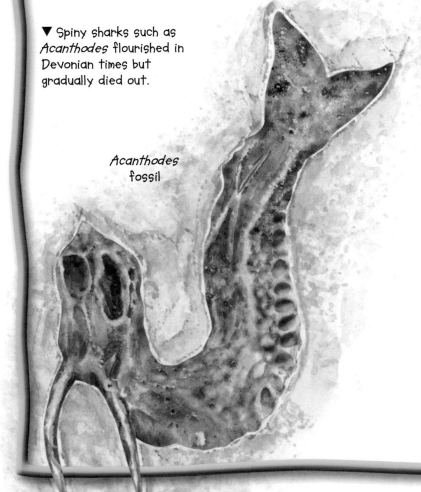

MILLIONS OF YEARS AGO	PERIOD	ERA
2 0	QUATERNARY	CENOZOIC ERA
23 20	NEOGENE	
	PALEOGENE	
65	CRETACEOUS	MESOZOIC ERA
145	JURASSIC	
199	TRIASSIC	
251	PERMIAN	PALEOZOIC ERA
299	CARBONIFEROUS	
359	DEVONIAN	
416	SILURIAN	
443	ORDOVICIAN	
488	CAMBRIAN	
540		

▲ The geological timescale spans the history of the Earth. This vast amount of time is broken down into eras, and then into time periods. By studying fossils from different periods we can see how abundant life was through prehistory.

As we find more fossils, the gaps or 'missing links' in the history of life are filled, and we identify more and more **extinctions.** Fossils show how whole groups of prehistoric living things started, spread and became common, then faded away. For example, there are many kinds of reptiles alive today, such as crocodiles, snakes, lizards and turtles. But other reptiles, such as dinosaurs, pterosaurs and ichthyosaurs, are long extinct.

Glossopteris fossil

▲ *Glossopteris* or Gondwana tree once covered huge areas, but disappeared.

▼ Ichthyosaurs became extinct with the dinosaurs, 65 million years ago.

Ichthyosaur fossil

Fossils also reveal that during some time periods, life was very varied, with lots of new species appearing and others dying out. At other times, plants and animals were less numerous and varied, with fewer new species evolving and lower numbers of extinctions.

▼ *Acanthostega* was one of the first four-legged land creatures.

Acanthostega fossil

◄ The extinct fish *Tiktaalik* shows a link between fish and land animals.

Tiktaalik fossil

Mass extinctions

At times in the Earth's history there have been mass extinctions, also called extinction events. Huge numbers of living things died out in a short time, usually less than a few thousand years. In some cases over half of all animals and plants disappeared.

▶ These are just a few of the millions of animals and plants that died out during mass extinctions.

ORDOVICIAN–SILURIAN
450–443 million years ago

Endoceras:
A type of mollusc

CAMBRIAN–ORDOVICIAN
488 million years ago

Pikaia:
An eel–like creature with a rod–like spinal column

The Cambrian–Ordovician mass extinction was 488 million years ago. It marked the change from the time span called the Cambrian Period to the next one, the Ordovician Period. Among the victims were many kinds of trilobites and lampshells, a kind of shellfish.

The Ordovician–Silurian mass extinction happened 450–443 million years ago, in two bursts. All life was in the sea at that time. Many types of shellfish, echinoderms (starfish, sea urchins and relatives) and corals died out.

▶ Mass extinctions show as dips in the variety of living things throughout prehistoric time.

Cambrian–Ordovician

Ordovician–Silurian

| 600 | 500 | 400 | Time (million years ago) |

CRETACEOUS-TERTIARY
65 million years ago

Triceratops:
One of the last dinosaurs

The Late Devonian mass extinction included several bursts 365-359 million years ago. Corals, trilobites and several groups of fish disappeared. It was the end of the 'Age of Fishes'.

LATE DEVONIAN
365-359 million years ago

TRIASSIC-JURASSIC
200 million years ago

Placodus:
A marine reptile

Dunkleosteus:
An armoured fish

The Triassic–Jurassic mass extinction occurred 200 million years ago. The main groups affected included many sea creatures, amphibians, and certain types of reptiles, including some early dinosaurs.

The Cretaceous-Tertiary mass extinction, 65 million years ago, is the most famous. It saw the extinction of the dinosaurs, as well as many other animals and plants. More than two-thirds of all species died out. The cause may have been a meteorite that smashed into Earth, setting off earthquakes, tsunamis and volcanoes, and causing rapid climate change.

Number of families

800

0

Late Devonian

Triassic–Jurassic

Cretaceous–Tertiary

200

100

0

The biggest of all

The most massive of all mass extinctions was the Permian-Triassic or end-of Permian event, 251 million years ago. Also known as the 'Great Dying' it saw vast losses with more than four-fifths of all Earth's species wiped out.

The 'Great Dying' was probably caused by the same combination of reasons as several other mass extinctions. These included volcanic eruptions, earthquakes and tsunamis. They were probably set off by the continents drifting into new positions, with accompanying changes in sea levels, ocean currents, wind patterns, rainfall and temperature.

The changes that probably caused mass extinctions were very complicated because of the way species depend on each other. If a particular plant could not cope with the changes and died out, then the animals that fed on it were also affected, as were the predators that fed on them. The balance of nature was upset and extinctions followed.

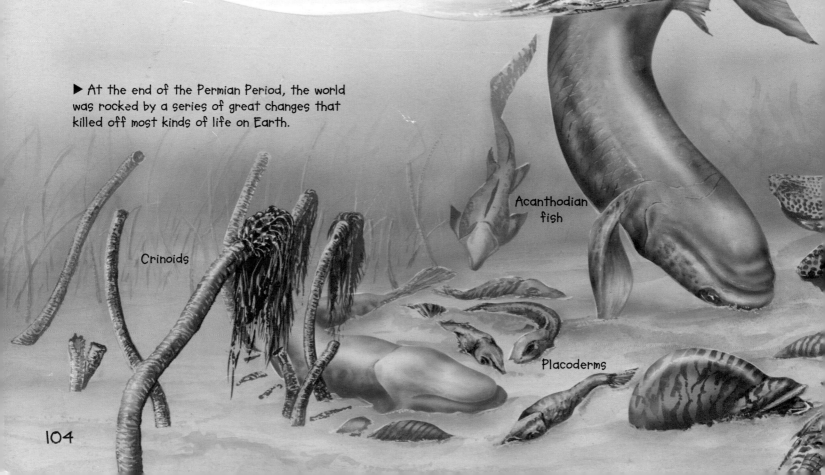

▶ At the end of the Permian Period, the world was rocked by a series of great changes that killed off most kinds of life on Earth.

Crinoids

Acanthodian fish

Placoderms

Mass extinctions upset some habitats more than others. In many of these events, including the Permian-Triassic one, most losses were marine life. Especially affected were tiny sea plants and creatures that formed the floating 'soup' of life known as plankton.

Diictodon

Lystrosaurus

Gorgonops

Mass extinctions were not total disasters. Afterwards, fewer species meant less competition. So there were chances and opportunities for a surge of evolution and new species. Just 20 million years after the Permian-Triassic 'Great Dying', the first dinosaurs were prowling the land while early pterosaurs flapped through the skies.

Corals

Trilobites

Ages of ice

Over the past few million years there have been several extinctions linked to more than a dozen ice ages. The first of these started around 2.6 million years ago and the last one faded just 15,000–10,000 years ago. These cold times are called glaciations, and the warmer periods between – like the one today – are interglacials.

An example of an extinct ice age species is the sabre-tooth cat *Smilodon*. There were perhaps five species of *Smilodon* starting around 2.5 million years ago. The last one, dying out only 10,000 years ago, was *Smilodon fatalis*.

▲ Last of the ice age sabre-tooth cats, *Smilodon* lived in the Americas and was as big as the largest big cat of today, the Siberian tiger.

Hundreds of other ice age animals have died out in the past 25,000 years. They include the woolly rhino, woolly mammoth, cave bear, dire wolf, and various kinds of horses, deer, camels, llamas, beavers, ground sloths, and even mice and rats.

Many of these large animals disappeared during a fairly short time period of 15,000–10,000 years ago. This happened especially across northern lands in North America, Europe and Asia. What was the cause of such widespread losses?

Two main reasons have been suggested for the recent ice age extinctions. One is rapid natural climate change. As the weather warmed up, some big animals could not evolve fast enough or travel to cooler areas. The woolly mammoth and woolly rhino, for example, may have overheated.

The second reason is the spread of humans. As the climate warmed, ice sheets and glaciers melted, and people moved north into new areas. Big animals such as mammoths were hunted for food, as shown in Stone Age cave paintings. Others, such as cave bears, were killed because they were dangerous.

▼ Low sea levels during ice ages allowed people to spread from eastern Asia to North America.

▶ Stone Age people probably trapped and killed mammoths, which would have provided them with food for weeks.

Keeping a record

In ancient times, people travelled little and did not record details of nature, so extinctions were hard to identify. From the 1500s, people began to explore the world, study living things and discover new species. They then hunted, shot, ate or collected them – some to extinction.

Spectacular examples of historical extinction are the elephant birds of Madagascar. There were several species of these giant, flightless birds, similar to ostriches but larger. The biggest stood 3 metres tall and weighed more than 450 kilograms.

▲ People exploring remote areas brought back tales of fanciful beasts – perhaps the result of several real creatures that explorers mixed up.

All elephant birds were extinct by the 1500s. People not only hunted them, but also collected and cooked their huge eggs, more than 35 centimetres in length.

▼ Elephant birds evolved on the island of Madagascar with no big predators to threaten them – until humans arrived.

Steller's sea cow was 8 metres long

▲ Extinctions of large creatures continued through recent centuries.

Bluebuck lived in small herds

Great auks once numbered millions

There is a long list of other animal species that went extinct even before 1900. They include the tall New Zealand ground birds called moas (by 1500), the huge European cow known as the auroch (probably 1630s), the North Pacific Steller's sea cow (1760s), the Southern African bluebuck antelope (around 1800) and the Atlantic penguin-like great auk (1850s).

I DON'T BELIEVE IT!

The huge moa of New Zealand was 4 metres tall. It was hunted by the enormous Haast's eagle, the biggest known eagle, which became extinct by 1400.

Many plants are also recorded as going extinct during this time. They include the Rio myrtle tree from South America (about 1820s), the string tree from the Atlantic island of St Helena (1860s) and the Indian kerala tree (1880s).

◄ St Helena ebony is a shrub that is being rescued from the brink of extinction.

Gathering pace

Over the last 100 years, the rate of extinction has speeded up greatly. More kinds of living things are disappearing than ever before. This is due mainly to human activity such as cutting down forests, habitat loss as natural areas are changed for farmland and houses, hunting, collecting rare species, and releasing chemicals into the environment.

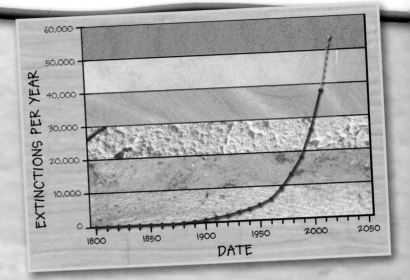

▲ The estimated extinction rate is rocketing as we find out about more threatened species every year.

▶ The spectacled bear of South America's Andes Mountains faces many threats, including the logging of its forest home.

One of the first extinctions to receive lots of publicity around the world was the Caribbean monk seal in the 1950s. It was hunted for its oil and meat, and to stop it eating the fish that people wanted to catch. From 2003, expeditions tried to find it again but gave up after five years.

▲ The last confirmed sightings of Caribbean monk seals were southeast of the island of Jamaica in 1952.

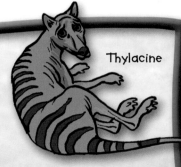

Thylacine

Other animal extinctions of the last 100 years include the thylacine and the Japanese sea lion. The last thylacine died of neglect in a zoo in Hobart, Tasmania in 1936, while the last Japanese sea lion was seen in 1974. Many plant species have also died out in the last 100 years, including the Cuban holly (1950s), the cry violet or cry pansy in France (1950s) and the woolly begonia of Malaysia (1960s).

With each passing year scientists explore, identify and record more living species in more detail than ever before. As we study and list all of these new plants and animals, we have a greater chance of discovering when one goes extinct.

▼ The Bosavi silky cuscus is a rarity – a new species discovered in Papua New Guinea.

FIND THAT SEAL!

You will need:
paper   pens

Imagine you are on an expedition to search for the Caribbean monk seal. Make a list of the equipment you would need. Binoculars, cameras, sketch pad, sound recorder… You need evidence, so don't forget specimen bottles for some of the seal's hair, or its urine or droppings!

Too many to disappear

The passenger pigeon was once extremely common. Flocks of millions flew around North America, darkening the skies as they passed. Before Europeans arrived in North America, native people caught the pigeons for their meat and feathers. This was on a small scale and happened for centuries without affecting the overall number of birds.

With the arrival of Europeans, especially from about 1700, came many changes. The new settlers altered the land from natural habitats to farms, roads and towns. Habitat loss soon gathered pace, and people also began to catch the pigeons for a cheap supply of food.

▼ Today, birds such as these city starlings seem too numerous to vanish. But we cannot be sure how they will fare in the future.

▶ Passenger pigeons became big business, with hunters shooting and trappers netting the birds to sell their meat in cities.

▲ Famous hunter, naturalist and artist John James Audobon painted passenger pigeons. He once said one flock was 'still passing in undiminished numbers... for three days'.

By the 1850s, the hunters and trappers noticed that passenger pigeon numbers had started to fall. But the killing continued. Some people tried to raise the pigeons in captivity, but the birds could only breed and thrive in very large flocks. Kept in small groups, they did not eat well or breed. They may have also suffered from a bird illness called Newcastle disease.

By 1900, the passenger pigeon had just about disappeared in the wild. The last one in captivity, Martha, died in Cincinnati Zoo, Ohio, USA in 1914. With her went one of the most numerous birds that ever existed.

I DON'T BELIEVE IT!

Martha, the last passenger pigeon, was named after Martha Washington, wife of the first US president George Washington. There are several statues and memorials to Martha (the pigeon), including one at Cincinnati Zoo.

▲ Passenger pigeons did not survive well in captivity. When the last one died in 1914, it was mounted or 'stuffed' at the Smithsonian Institute.

Island extinctions

Hawaii

CUBA

▼ Tiny islands in vast oceans around the world are 'hotbeds' of extinctions.

Galapagos Islands

Cuban solenodon — this shrew-like creature has not been seen since 2008

Hawaiian black mamo — gone by the 1920s

PACIFIC OCEAN

Galapagos damselfish — became extinct during the 1980s

SOUTHERN ATLANTIC OCEAN

In the past few centuries, more than two-thirds of living things becoming extinct have lived on islands. Islands can support only small numbers of a particular species, so there is a higher risk of dying out. Each island also has its own particular conditions, to which species adapt over thousands of years. If conditions change, for example, when people arrive, the local wild species may be threatened.

Island plants and animals are also at great risk from introduced species — those brought by people. These introduced species include sheep, goats, cows, foxes, stoats, mice, rats, cats and dogs. They start to compete with the local species for food, or prey on them, or steal their nest sites, or give them diseases — or all of these.

PACIFIC OCEAN

MAURITIUS

I esser bilby – not seen on the island continent of Australia since the 1950s

AUSTRALIA

INDIAN OCEAN

Mauritius dodo – disappeared by the 1690s

THE DODO LIVES AGAIN!

You will need:
sheet of card   scissors   coloured pens
sticky tape   elastic

Cut out a face mask in the shape of a dodo's head and beak and colour it as shown (left). Find out from books or the Internet about the noises a dodo made. Now you can try to bring the dodo back to life!

Perhaps the most famous example of any extinct animal is the dodo. This flightless, turkey-sized bird lived on Mauritius in the Indian Ocean, ate fruit and nested on the ground. It had no natural predators or enemies. Then people arrived with animals that hunted it, its eggs and its chicks. By 1700, the dodo was gone, leading to the saying 'dead as a dodo'.

At least 50 bird species from the Hawaiian Islands are extinct. This affected other wildlife. Some of the birds fed on nectar and carried pollen so that flowers could breed. Others ate fruits and spread the seeds in their droppings. Without the birds, some of these plants become extinct. When one species disappears, then another that depends on it dies out, it is known as co-extinction.

What's happening today?

In the natural world today, extinction rates are shooting up due to a huge variety of causes. Scientists call this another time of mass extinction.

The main cause of today's extinctions is habitat loss and degradation (changing natural habitats for the worse). The number of people in the world is rising fast and they need land for their houses, farms, factories, roads and leisure, leaving less wild areas.

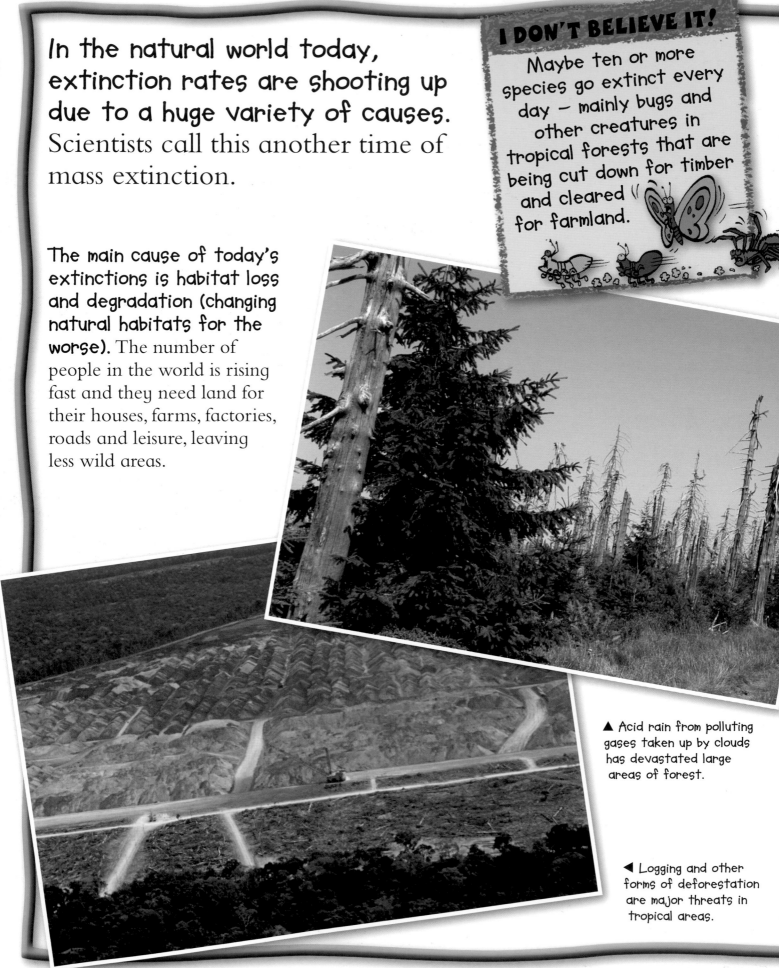

▲ Acid rain from polluting gases taken up by clouds has devastated large areas of forest.

◄ Logging and other forms of deforestation are major threats in tropical areas.

Other causes include pollution and hunting for food or trophies. There is also the collecting of species for displays, introduced species, and diseases that spread from domestic animals and farm plants to wild species. As the early signs of global warming and climate change become more marked, these will also have huge effects on habitats and push species towards extinction.

▲ The baiji is probably now extinct. Some people hope it survives in backwaters of the Yangtze and nearby rivers. There are rare sightings, but for the time being, no proof.

In 2007, a search in China failed to find any baijis, or Yangtze river dolphins. This species was threatened for many reasons, including dams built across its rivers, pollution, hunting and the overfishing of its natural prey.

▼ Now extinct, golden toads were probably victims of global warming and increased human activity in their natural habitats.

On the brink

Every year, wildlife experts make lists of animals and plants that are threatened with extinction. These are known as the IUCN 'Red Lists', and every year, they grow longer.

► Symbols indicate if a species is threatened or not, ranging from LC meaning Least Concern, to EX meaning Extinct.

QUIZ

Which of these amphibians is threatened with extinction?
1. Lungless Mexican salamander
2. South African ghost frog
3. Betic midwife toad
4. Chinese giant salamander
5. Darwin frog

Answer: All of them, plus thousands of others

One of the most endangered groups of animals is the rhinos. There are only five rhino species and all are in huge trouble. The black, Javan and Sumatran rhinos are listed as 'critically endangered'. They will become extinct in 20–50 years unless massive efforts are made to save them.

White rhino

▼ All rhinos need action to save them. Most numerous is the white rhino, with less than 20,000.

Sumatran rhino

Javan rhino

Black rhino

A larger group, with many species at risk of extinction, is the amphibians. More than half of the 6000-plus species are threatened. A terrible problem is the new fungus infection called chytrid disease. Recent amphibian extinctions include the gastric-brooding frog of Australia, which swallowed its eggs so the tadpoles could grow in its stomach. It died out in the 1980s.

▶ Baby gastric-brooding frogs emerged from their mother's mouth. Many other species of frogs, toads and newts are also under threat.

You cannot get closer to extinction than only one remaining individual. The café marron bush grew on the island of Rodrigues in the Indian Ocean, but finally only one bush was left. Scientists at Kew Gardens, London took cuttings from it in the 1980s and grew them into bushes. Now some are being taken back to Rodrigues.

▲ The world's largest flower, rafflesia, is now extremely rare.

Indian rhino

Coral reefs are among the world's richest places for wildlife. But these whole habitats may become extinct in the next 100–200 years. They are in great danger from threats such as global warming, pollution, water cloudiness and acidity upsetting the delicate natural balance between their species.

▶ Due to global warming, coral reefs may become 'bleached' and die.

Saved just in time

To save an almost extinct species takes time, effort and money. This means studying it and its habitat, its contact with other species and finding out how many are left. Scientists assess its needs through field studies – in the wild – and also captive studies. They establish what it eats, where it nests or which soil it likes, so that places can be put aside.

Rescuing a threatened animal or plant from extinction also means saving its habitat. Without somewhere natural and safe to live, the species cannot thrive in the wild. Otherwise, even if it is saved, it will always be limited to a park, zoo or similar place, and be extinct in the wild.

Female

Male

▲ Through a huge conservation effort, the numbers of ladybird spiders in Great Britain have risen.

▼ In North America, movements of very rare black-footed ferrets are studied by radio transmitter collars.

It's less use people coming to an area from far away, and trying to save a species, than local people getting involved. The locals need to have input into the rescue effort. Through ecotourism, visitors can see rare wildlife without damaging it or the habitat and pay money, which is put towards conservation efforts.

SAVE OUR SPIDER

You will need:
large sheet of paper
coloured pens

Spiders may not be everyone's favourite animal, but they deserve saving as much as other species. Find out about the ladybird spider, which is almost extinct in Britain. Make a colourful poster telling people why it should not be allowed to die out.

◀ Elephant safaris allow paying tourists to get close to rare rhinos without disturbing them too much.

Saving one 'flagship' or 'headline' species from extinction can help to save whole habitats. Such species usually appeal to the public because they are big and powerful, like tigers and mountain gorillas, or cute and fluffy, like giant pandas and golden lion tamarins.

▼ Setting up wildlife parks and nature reserves helps not only the headline species, such as these gorillas, but all the plants and animals living there.

Should we care?

Why should we care if a species goes extinct? Especially if it is some small bug in a remote forest, or a worm on the seabed. Does it really matter or affect us in any way?

Many people think that all animals and plants have a right to be here on Earth. We should not destroy nature for little reason. If we let species die out, it shows we do not care for our surroundings and the natural world. These types of reasons are known as moral and ethical arguments.

There are medical reasons for saving species. Researchers may discover that a particular type of plant or animal is the source of a new wonder drug to cure illness. If it had gone extinct, we would never know this. Other species can be used for medical research into diseases such as cancers.

Scientific reasons to prevent species dying out are also important. Extinction reduces biodiversity, which is the variety of living things necessary for the balance of nature. The genes in certain animals or plants could be used in GM, genetic modification, perhaps to improve our farm crops and make our farm animals healthier.

There are also traditional and cultural reasons for caring about extinction. Some endangered species are important to ethnic groups and tribes for their history, ceremonies, myths and special foods. People should not come to an area from afar with new ways of living and cause habitat loss, introduce new animals, plants and diseases and kill off local species.

▲ The Florida panther is an extremely rare subspecies of cougar, or mountain lion. If it dies out, there will still be other cougars elsewhere. So would its disappearance matter?

I DON'T BELIEVE IT!

In the 1800s, European explorers in Australia captured now-extinct creatures including pig-footed bandicoots. But when the explorers got lost and hungry, they ate the bandicoots.

Gone forever?

People once thought that extinction is forever, but future science may change this view. The idea of bringing extinct animals or plants back to life can be seen through films such as *Jurassic Park*. Scientists use a species' eggs, its genes or its genetic material such as DNA (de-oxyribonucleic acid).

▲ In the *Jurassic Park* stories, dinosaurs were recreated from their preserved genes and hatched in egg incubators.

▼ Why the Pyrenean ibex died out is unclear, but it may have been the result of infectious diseases.

In 2009, a baby Pyrenean ibex, a subspecies of the goat-like Spanish ibex, was born. Its mother was a goat but its genes came from one of the last Pyrenean ibexes, which had died out by 2000. The young ibex was a genetic copy but it showed what might be possible in future.

QUIZ

Put these species in order of when they became extinct, from longest ago to most recent.
1. Quagga
2. Dodo
3. Neanderthal humans
4. Baiji (Yangtze river dolphin)
5. Woolly mammoth

Answers:
3. About 30,000 years ago
5. Around 10,000 years ago
2. By 1700 1. 1883 4. By 2007 (probably)

EXTINCT

To revive extinct species, there are many problems to solve in genetic engineering, altering DNA, cloning and similar methods. However scientists are taking samples of DNA and other material from all kinds of sources, such as frozen mammoths, dodo bones, the dead seeds of extinct plants, and even long-gone humans, to carry out experiments and see what can be done.

▲ The Barbary lion of North Africa was thought to be extinct from the 1920s, but genetic tests have revealed several living in zoos.

▼ The Quagga Project selects and breeds the most quagga-like zebras over many generations.

The quagga, which went extinct in 1883, was a subspecies of the plains zebra of southern Africa. It had zebra stripes on its front half but was plain brown at the rear. The Quagga Project aims to 'breed back' quaggas. This is done by choosing plains zebras that look most like quaggas, and allowing them to mate. Gradually, after several generations, the young of plains zebras should look more and more like quaggas.

INDEX

Entries in **bold** refer to main subject entries. Entries in *italics* refer to illustrations.

ACKNOWLEDGEMENTS

All artworks are from the Miles Kelly Artwork Bank

The publishers would like to thank the following sources for the use of their photographs:

t = top, b = bottom, l = left, r = right, c = centre

Alamy Page 14 Tom Uhlman; 32(t) AGStockUSA, Inc.; 97(br) John Glover; 98 Mary Evans Picture Library; 121(c) Picture Press; 124(t) Photos 12

Corbis Page 8 NASA/Reuters; 13(c) Bettmann; 16(b) Klaus Hackenberg/zefa; 18(t) Jean-Paul Pelissier/Reuters; 19(t) Dean Conger; 22 Arctic-Images; 23(bl) Gideon Mendel; 25 Olivier Maire/eps, (tr) Phil Schermeister; 26 Yann Arthus – Bertrand, (bl) Vivianne Moos; 28 Gene Blevins/LA Daily News; 29(b) Ron Sanford; 32(b) Ed Young; 34(t) Mike Segar/Reuters, (b) Desmond Boylan/Reuters; 35(t) Martin Harvey; 39(t) Brian S. Turner/Frank Lane Picture Agency; 41(c) Kate Davidson/epa; 45(main) Neil Farrin/JAI; 45(t) Jeffrey L Rotman; 47(t) Reuters; (c) Yann Arthus-Bertrand; 52(b) Martin Harvey/Gallo Images; 60 Frans Lanting; 62 Fernando Bengaechea/Beateworks; 64(t) Karen Kasmauski; 65(b) George Steinmetz; 66(t) momatiuk-Eastcott; 69 Owen Franken; 71(b) Keren Su; 73(t) Jeffrey L Rofman; 80(b) Theo Allots; 81 Martin Harvey; 84 Natalie Fobes; 85 Theo Allots; 93(t) Jonathan Blair; 95(br) Corbis; 117(t) Alex Hofford; (b) Patricia Fogden; 121(b) Martin Harvey

Dreamstime.com Page 89(tr) South China tiger Trix1428; 112(c) Photoinjection; 119(b) Naluphoto

F.H. Idzerda Page 89(c)

FLPA Page 10 Tui De Roy/Minden Pictures; 33(b) Ulrich Niehoff/Imagebroker; 40(b) Katherine Feng/Globio/Minden Pictures; 48 Frans Lanting; 54 Winfried Wisniewski; 63 Panda Photo; 74(b) Tui De Roy/Minden Pictures; 75(t) Linda Lewis; 76 David Hosking; 79 Flip Nicklin/Minden Pictures; 80(t) David Hosking; 82 Katherine Feng/Globio/Minden Pictures; 96 Gerard Lacz; 124(b) Simon Littlejohn/Minden Pictures

Fotolia Page 13(b) schaltwerk.de; 30 David Kesti; 36(t) Steve Estvanik; 37(t) Olga Alexandrova; 38(b) Ennoy Engelhardt; 44(b) MiklG; 89(cr) Sumatran tiger Vladimir Wrangel, (br) Malayan tiger Kitch Bain, (br) Indochinese tiger Judy Whitton; 92(bl) clearviewstock; 97(c); 116(t) sisu; 119(c) Jefery

Getty Images Page 15 China Photos/Stringer; 19(b); 36(b) Per-Anders Pettersson; 43(tl) Dimas Ardian/Stringer; 53 Art Wolfe; 72(b) Karen Kasmauski; 83(t) National Geographic; 108(b) National Geographic; 125(t) AFP

Kew images Page 95(cl) RBGKew

Naturepl.com Page 70 Luiz Claudio Marigo; 75(b) Andrew Murray; 110–111 Eric Baccega; 120 Andrew Harrington

NHPA Page 52(t) Jonathan & Angela Scott; 65(t) Mark Carwardine; 68(b) Jonathan & Angela Scott; 73(b) Martin Harvey; 74(t) Martin Wendler; 111(b) Bruce Beehler; 119(t) Photoshot

Oxford Scientific Page 64(b) Newman & Associates

Photolibrary.com Page 72(t) Nick Gordon; 92(c) Paul Nevin; 93(br) Stouffer Productions; 109 Howard Rice; 122–123 Purestock

Rex Features Page 99 Icon/Everett

Save the Rhino International Page 56(t)

Science Photo Library Page 24 Victor Habbick Visions; 86–87 Richard Bizley; 125(b) Philippe Psaila

Sunshine Solar Page 23(cr)

Topfoto Page 108(t) Artmedia/HIP; 112(b) The Granger Collection; 113(t) The Granger Collection; (b) Topham Picturepoint

www.ecozone.co.uk Page 33(t)

www.firebox.com Page 21

www.ICRF.co.uk Page 83(b) John F. Binns

All other photographs are from: Corel, digitalSTOCK, digitalvision, ImageState, iStockphoto.com, John Foxx, PhotoAlto, PhotoDisc, PhotoEssentials, PhotoPro, Stockbyte

Every effort has been made to acknowledge the source and copyright holder of each picture. Miles Kelly Publishing apologises for any unintentional errors or omissions.